To: Steve

Enjoy and I hope this
is a blessing to you.

-Brennan

Brennan Farrell

The Smart Ministry®

A Practical Guide
To Executing God's Plans

BRENNAN FARRELL

www.xulonpress.com

Dedication

To my wife, Britney:

Thank you for being strong where I am weak,
For being a person of truth, character, and grace,
And for being my partner in all we have been through.

I love you.
I am blessed beyond measure to call you mine.

Table of Contents

Foreword

Over the last 40 years, the Lord has called me to serve His Kingdom as a missionary, pastor, professor, and counselor. In my early years as a missionary in Western Alaska, living in the community of Bethel on the Kuskokwim River, there were very few tools and resources available to a young man for ministry besides the Word of God. I learned then and afterwards during my twelve years as a missionary in Zimbabwe, Africa, that ministry efforts can benefit from practical insights and strategies.

As I reflect upon my time as the Principal of a Bible College in Harare, leading the development of the first Christian Counseling Center in Zimbabwe, or pastoring a growing multicultural congregation in America, I have learned that developing a strategic plan built on the solid foundation of biblical truth has allowed me to not only help bear fruit, but as Jesus said, bear *"fruit that will last" (John 15:16).*

In this very well written and carefully developed guide to ministry development, Brennan Farrell has provided a gift that will benefit every reader. *The Smart Ministry* outlines 12 Principles that will help any Christian minister strategically plan and operate their ministry in order to increase their contribution to the advancement of God's Kingdom. A refreshing element of *The Smart Ministry* is Brennan's writing style, which engages the reader by sharing much more than statistics or figures. He has woven in meaningful examples of how successful businesses and ministries have used the 12 Principles as tools to positively impact people's lives, adding an extra level of authenticity to his insights. As another valuable component of the book, *The Smart Ministry* provides unique "Action Questions" that help the reader reflect upon the material, challenge their current ways of thinking, and implement ideas that will help the development of their ministry for the glory of God. In total, *The Smart Ministry* is a tool that can benefit every Christian minister, no matter their role or where they are in their walk with God.

I have known Brennan and his family for over a decade and can testify to his love for the Lord and passion to be the best steward possible with what God has blessed him with. It was Helen Keller who made this insightful declaration: *"Life is either a daring adventure or nothing at all."* Brennan is pursuing the *"daring adventure"* and has provided a helpful tool for others to do the same.

Dr. James J. Seymour
Senior Pastor: North Haven Church
Associate Professor: Saint Augustine's University
Missionary: Alaska and Zimbabwe

About the Author

After graduating from Elon University's Martha and Spencer Love School of Business, Brennan worked in project management and later served as Sales Director at SPS, a global IT solutions company. At the publication of this book, he is serving as the VP of Professional Services for eWater Advantage®, a sustainable technology firm. Brennan has a heart for Kingdom-based work, and has been called to use the platform of business to glorify God and to help fulfill the Great Commission.

Over the course of his career, Brennan recognized that while formal education and hands-on experience are great teachers, self-education can be a unique way to continuously maximize workplace productivity. Through extensive self-education, in addition to nearly 10 years of being immersed in competitive business environments, Brennan has created a unique presentation for understanding how top organizations thrive and generate results.

The Smart Ministry focuses on 12 leadership and management principles that will help every Christian ministry maximize its potential to impact people's lives for the Gospel. This book is a resource that encompasses the knowledge and experiences of many different subject matter experts and successful organizations, designed to elevate Christian ministries to new heights of operational efficiency and effectiveness. Additionally, with each book purchase, 51% of Brennan's proceeds will be contributed towards local and global outreach projects that serve others in Jesus' name. To learn more about how *The Smart Ministry* is impacting lives, please visit www.thesmartministry.com.

Featured Organizations

T he Smart Ministry includes over 40 custom statements written specifically for this book, generated by leaders from the "Featured Organizations" listed below. Part 1 of the book provides examples of how successful businesses that operate under Christian values use each principle within their organization. Part 1 also provides examples of how successful Christian ministries use each principle to impact people's lives for the Gospel.

FEATURED ORGANIZATIONS	STATEMENTS PROVIDED BY:
ANTHONY & COMPANY	Jim Anthony, Founder and CEO
BANDWIDTH™	Henry Kaestner, Co-founder and Executive Chairman
CEDAR CREEK CHURCH	Lee Powell, Lead Pastor
DOULOS PARTNERS	David Johnson, Executive Director
FELLOWSHIP OF CHRISTIAN ATHLETES	Johnny Evans, Eastern NC Director
FORREST FIRM	James Forrest, Founder
GLOBAL MEDIA OUTREACH	Michelle Diedrich, Executive Director Jordan Stone, Global Catalyst Kathy Gray, Marketing Manager
INTERNATIONAL LEADERSHIP INSTITUTE	Kyle Philips, USA Director
LIVING WATER INTERNATIONAL	Jonathan Wiles, VP for Program Excellence
PARTNERS INTERNATIONAL	Larry Andrews, President and CEO
SAMARITAN'S PURSE®	Ron Wilcox, COO
SOUTHLAND CHRISTIAN CHURCH	Chris Hahn, Lead Executive Pastor
STORR OFFICE ENVIRONMENTS	Tom Vande Guchte, CEO
THE JESUS FILM PROJECT®	Josh Newell, Director of Marketing and Communications
THE RESET AGENCY	Dave Jones, Co-founder
THE SUMMIT CHURCH	David Thompson, Lead Pastor of Executive Leadership Daniel Simmons, Executive Pastor of Campuses

Overview, Purpose, and Benefits

We are living in an unprecedented era of information availability, technology innovation, and advanced means of communicating. The website, www.theemergingfuture.com, states that in five years, technology will be 32 times more advanced than it is today. In ten years, 1,000 times more advanced and in twenty years, 1,000,000 times more advanced! Whatever the future brings, we can be assured that emerging technologies, trends, and the new paradigms they create will continually change the way we live and how we interact with others.

The buzzword today for innovative products or new technologies is the word "smart." It is common for most people to have "smart phones," "smart TVs," "smart cars," and a host of other smart technologies that will continue to be innovated upon as time progresses. The world is changing at a rapid pace, and Christian ministries have the option to choose how they respond to these changes in order to maximize their potential to help advance God's Kingdom. A "smart ministry" **strategically operates** their organization, while remaining aligned with God's Word, for the sake of impacting people's lives for the Gospel.

For nearly a decade, I have been part of businesses that provide cutting edge solutions for customers in a variety of different markets. God has called me to be a "Marketplace Christian,"[1] and to use business as my pulpit to help shine the light of Jesus in the secular world. As a Christian businessman, I recognize my daily need for God's wisdom, favor, and direction—however, I also know that God calls me to take action by using the intellect and resources He has given me. The strategies, tactics, and principles I've used in business are all under God's authority, and my need for Him to bless my actions is no different than the need of the Christian minister in a church or non-profit setting. Everything we see, don't see, understand, and don't understand belongs to God, and He can use it all for His purposes and for His glory. He is completely, perfectly, and eternally sovereign over all.

12 Operating Principles of Successful Organizations

Over the course of my career, I've learned there are 12 Principles that are essential for any business to understand in order to be successful. The eye-opening revelation, however, was discovering the relevance and importance of each principle for Christian ministries as well. Equipped with the knowledge of the 12 Principles, I met with pastors, PhD's, theological experts, missionaries, and evangelists to validate this idea. The conclusion in every discussion was the same. While there are empirical differences between businesses and ministries, there are empirical similarities as well. It is because of the similarities that this book was written. *The Smart Ministry* is the first book to show *why* the 12 Principles are important to understand and *how* they can be used within the key operating contexts of any Christian ministry.

---

[1] Ed Silvoso, *Anointed For Business* (Ventura, Regal Books, 2002), 36.

The following list outlines the 12 Principles of *The Smart Ministry*:

1. **Vision and Execution** – Understanding *why* your ministry exists, *what* it is striving to do, and *how* its goals will be achieved.
2. **Market Intelligence** – Acquiring and understanding essential information that will enable your outreach efforts to be as highly impactful as possible.
3. **Maximizing Credibility** – Maximizing the trustworthiness, integrity, and authenticity of your ministry.
4. **Problem Awareness** – Understanding the dynamics of the problems your ministry intends to solve.
5. **Problem Implications** – Using wisdom and experience to anticipate consequences before they happen.
6. **Solution Benefits** – Creating solutions that deliver meaningful benefits in any situation.
7. **Strategic Positioning** – Leveraging your ministry's unique attributes to create value for others.
8. **Interest Generation** – Maximizing the opportunities your ministry can create to serve and partner with others.
9. **Creating Urgency** – Understanding how to motivate people to take action.
10. **Handling Objections** – Properly handling the two types of objections people have.
11. **Leveraging Testimonials** – Understanding how to leverage the power of sharing personal stories.
12. **Managing Relationships** – Understanding the importance of maximizing the quality of relationships.

The Theology

The theology of *The Smart Ministry* is based on the reality that there is one God who represents Himself in the form of three distinct Persons: God the Father, God the Son (Jesus Christ), and God the Holy Spirit. As part of the Holy Trinity, Jesus Christ came from Heaven to Earth nearly 2,000 years ago to sacrifice Himself for the sins of humanity, so that through belief in Him, our sins would be forgiven and our relationship with God would be restored. Any person who declares with their mouth that Jesus is Lord and believes in their heart that God raised Him from the dead (Romans 10:9), will be forgiven of their sins, filled with the Holy Spirit, and assured eternity in Heaven. We are saved by the grace of God.

The Purpose

God is sovereign over everything and there is nothing outside of His control. He can use anything to glorify His name, accomplish His will, and grow His church. The 12 Principles within *The Smart Ministry* are tools that will help every Christian ministry glorify God, accomplish His will, and do their part in bringing fulfillment to the Great Commission.

This book will provide your ministry with a strategic operating framework to help it function with maximum efficiency and effectiveness. **Why is this important?** Without a strategic operating framework that is aligned with God's Word, Christian ministries risk falling short of their potential to impact people's lives for the Gospel. Nearly 1,500 years ago, St. Augustine said something that defines what *The Smart Ministry* is all about: "Pray as if everything depends on God. Work as if everything depends on you." As Christians, God's desire for us is to do just that—have a total dependency upon Him while doing our part to accomplish His will. He could do it all Himself if He wanted—much better and much quicker than we ever could. However, God chooses to work through fault-filled, sinful beings—you and I—to accomplish things that have both temporal and eternal significance. He requires us to take action while still having full reliance upon Him.

We've all heard the saying, "Knowledge is power." A better way to say it would be, "The application of knowledge is power." *The Smart Ministry* suggests that the **application of knowledge *in obedience to God* is power**. Use this book as a guide to apply contemporary knowledge, in obedience to God, for His purposes and for His glory.

The Target Audience

There are over four million full-time Christian workers around the world.[2] This book is meant for every Christian worker who is either enrolled in seminary or who is part of a Christian ministry (church or non-profit) that desires to strategically develop their ministry in ways that are pleasing to God.

What is ministry development? Ministry development is using a strategic operating framework that is aligned with God's Word to impact people's lives for the Gospel. *The Smart Ministry* is **the** strategic operating framework.

The Smart Ministry will create value for you no matter your role or the phase that your ministry is in:

---

[2] http://www.thetravelingteam.org/stats, 2015

<u>For a New Ministry</u>

Are you part of a new ministry? If so, you will be experiencing many of the challenges one faces at the inception phase of a new business. This is also true if you are part of a new division of an existing ministry. One of the best things you can do when starting something new is to have a plan. Alan Lakein, well-known author on "time management" principles, once said, "Failing to plan is planning to fail." *The Smart Ministry* will help you plan and create a roadmap for success so that you can begin your efforts with as much confidence as possible.

<u>For a Discovering Ministry</u>

Are you trying to create your ministry's true identity but feel lost in uncertainty and lack of direction? Many businesses have an initial idea of why they exist and what they want to achieve, but then shift to another direction as time progresses. This process is described in the book, *The Entrepreneurial Mindset*, as "discovery-driven planning"[3] and is common when organizations are on the path towards discovering their unique purpose. You may be experiencing something similar in your ministry today. If you are facing uncertainties or struggling to create your ministry's true identity, this book will help you define why your ministry exists and what it desires to achieve.

<u>For a Hindered Ministry</u>

Are you part of a ministry that seems to have hit a growth-wall or challenging set of obstacles? If so, a renewed perspective on existing problems can create solutions that were present all along. *The Smart Ministry* will help you tackle problems, remove obstacles, and implement solutions that create long-term sustainable value for your ministry and others.

<u>For a Successful Ministry</u>

Has your ministry already achieved what you would define as "success"? If you are pleased with your ministry's current operation, but would like to investigate new ways to continuously improve, this book will be a valuable resource for you. *The Smart Ministry* will help you:

- Innovate in areas that are already strong.
- Improve in areas that are currently weak.
- Capitalize on unique service, outreach, and partnership opportunities.
- Be better equipped to handle difficult circumstances.

---

[3] Rita McGrath Gunther and Ivan MacMillan, *The Entrepreneurial Mindset* (Boston: Harvard Business School Press, 2000), 232.

The Benefits

I believe there are many ways that you and your ministry will benefit from reading this book, but allow me to list five. *The Smart Ministry*:

- Will enable your ministry to maximize its potential to impact people's lives for the Gospel.

- Is an applicable and valuable resource, regardless of your role or the phase your ministry is in.

- Will enable your ministry to understand and apply contemporary knowledge while remaining under the timeless authority of God.

- Will better position your ministry to raise the necessary funds to execute your vision and mission, regardless of the economic conditions you face in your city, state, or country.

- Will become your ministry partner, as 51% of my proceeds from book sales will be contributed towards global outreach projects that serve others in Jesus' name.

The Smart Ministry will help your ministry strengthen its operational efficiency and effectiveness, without compromising Scripture or reducing reliance upon God for faith, wisdom, and direction. This is the first book written that shows how understanding and applying this unique set of 12 Principles will benefit your ministry within each of its Five Key Contexts: Service Audience(s), Financial Partners, Volunteers, Strategic Partners, and Staff Members.

The Structure

Part 1 of *The Smart Ministry* focuses on *why* the 12 Principles are important to understand. This is accomplished through showing the "business logic" of the 12 Principles in order to validate their importance within the Five Key Contexts of every Christian ministry:

Five Key Contexts
Service Audience – People or organizations a ministry serves by providing solutions for various physical and/or spiritual needs they have.
Financial Partners – People or organizations that provide financial contributions to help a ministry operate and/or execute specific events, projects, or missions.
Volunteers – People that provide a ministry with their time, talents, and resources at no cost to help the ministry scale its operations.
Strategic Partners – People or organizations a ministry partners with to create unique capabilities or to capitalize on outreach opportunities.
Staff Members – People that operate a ministry and are responsible for executing its vision and mission.

Each chapter in Part 1 also references stories and case studies, told by Christian businessmen and ministry leaders that operate successful organizations—these are the "Featured Organizations" of *The Smart Ministry*. Additionally, you will read about personal experiences that outline why understanding and applying the 12 Principles have proved to be highly beneficial in my career.

Furthermore, each chapter in Part 1 includes a unique method of communicating why each principle is important for ministries to understand. This technique was developed by Toyota Motor Company and is known as the "5 Why's"—referred to in *The Smart Ministry* as "The *Why* Chain", which begins with a short statement followed by a series of "why" questions. The first "why" is asked based on the provided statement. The next "why" is asked based on the answer to the first "why" question. This process continues until the root understanding of the statement is uncovered. As Friedrich Nietzsche said, "If you know the why, you can live any how."

In addition to "The Why Chain", each chapter concludes with a visual diagram, a short poem called "Rhyme *for* Reason", and "Scriptural Application" from the Gospels. The purpose of these sections is to summarize the importance of each principle, in ways that are simple, unique, and memorable.

Part 2 is a built-in workbook containing "Action Questions" related to each principle, with space provided to write notes or ideas to be brainstormed upon individually and as a group. *The Smart Ministry* concludes with three appendixes. Appendix One provides 40 questions designed to show how you can utilize the 12 Principles to help frame and communicate the Gospel message. Appendix Two provides additional action questions coupled with over 60 "Featured Resources" that may be of value to your ministry's operations. Appendix Three outlines 15 lessons I've learned in business that can positively impact you as an individual in addition to your ministry as a whole.

Send-Off

The Smart Ministry was written for you, the Christian minister. My prayer is that God will use this book as a resource to help your ministry develop in ways that honor Him by leading others to the knowledge of His saving grace. Thank you for your partnership with *The Smart Ministry*.

Part 1: The "*Why*"
Understanding the 12 Principles

CHAPTER 1

Vision and Execution

"Vision without execution is hallucination." — *Thomas Edison*

An organization's **beliefs** and **values** determine *why* it exists, *what* it is striving to do, and *how* its goals will be achieved. They are influential in nearly every decision an organization makes, and can be considered the foundation of its vision, mission, and execution strategies.

Many organizations have trouble differentiating between their vision and mission. To some, they have a vision but no mission, or vice versa. To others, their vision and mission are the same. I would suggest that a vision and mission are distinctly different from each other, but they work together to help organizations create a sense of purpose and direction. An organization's vision and mission have little meaning, however, without an execution strategy designed to help it fulfill its purpose and achieve its goals.

Vision (The *Why*)

An organization's vision describes *why* it exists. This can be expressed in a statement that outlines its ultimate goal or what it wants to become. One way of creating a vision is to do what author Steven Covey teaches, which is to "start with the end in mind" by visualizing the desired end result and creating goals and strategies designed to help you get there. A vision statement outlines the highest level goal and/or desired outcome, and all other goals and objectives fall under and support it.

Dave Jones, Co-founder of The Reset Agency, describes vision this way:

> A vision statement is a vivid, idealized description of a desired outcome that inspires, energizes and helps you create a mental picture of your future. The Reset Agency's vision is to "Communicate the vision of every individual on the planet." We are a coaching firm that helps individuals and organizations realize their passions and purpose. Supporting this vision are core values that help shape The Reset Agency's daily actions and attitudes in addition to serving as a reflection of the priorities of our organization.

A vision statement should be simple, easy to understand, portable, short, inspiring, empowering, people oriented, memorable, and destination-driven by a God-inspired passion and purpose. Some of the best vision statements transcend a person's lifetime and stretch an organization to realize its dependency upon God for wisdom and favor. Vision (Hebrew, chazon) is derived from chazah, "to perceive, to foresee." It is sometimes a synonym for "dream." Vision is the future, while mission statements are the steps to accomplishing the vision, making them both different, however fulfilling complimentary purposes. When the vision and mission are aligned, backed by core values, individuals become unified with passion to create strategies and execute them in a way that turns dreams into reality.

Every business and ministry needs vision to steer their organization in the right direction, and when God is at its center, impossibilities are removed and achievements have no limit.

The Summit Church, located in Raleigh, North Carolina, has a vision to "plant 1,000 churches in our generation." This simple statement outlines The Summit Church's **ultimate goal**. Lead Pastor of Executive Leadership, David Thompson, said the following in support of his church's vision: "We desire to **become** a church that plants, influences, and serves other churches to such an extent that all people have a Gospel-centered and disciple-making church in their community."

An additional way to help describe *why* an organization exists can be summarized in a "core purpose" or "purpose statement," which provides further evidence of why an organization wants to achieve a certain goal or outcome.

Mission (The *What*)

A mission statement outlines *what* an organization is striving to do. More specifically, the impact it desires to make.

*From 2012-2015, eWater Advantage was discovering "the why" of our organization, which is now expressed in the following statement: "To positively impact people and the planet through innovative sustainability technologies." Through understanding why we exist, we are able to clearly articulate "**what**" our company is striving to do, represented in the following mission statement: "To provide our customers with technology solutions that reduce costs, lower operating risks, and increase standards of personal health, safety, and environmental responsibility."*

eWater provides "Engineered Water" technology solutions that are designed to reduce our customer's reliance upon chemicals for cleaning, sanitizing, deodorizing, and disinfecting. eWater's mission statement communicates the benefits that we are able to offer our customers: reduced costs (compared to conventional chemical use), lower operating risks (by eliminating risks associated with chemical use), and increased standards of per-sonal health, safety, and environmental responsibility (results of chemical removal from facilities). This mission is something we strive to accomplish in every customer engage-ment and it summarizes the value we are able to offer.

To help further differentiate between a vision and mission, here is an example from the ministry world. Ministries will sometimes conduct a "vision trip" to ensure that the purpose of a future "mission trip" is clear. It would not make much sense for a mission trip to precede a vision trip. Having a vision first determines *why* the mission trip is needed, which clarifies *what* the ministry will strive to do (mission) and *how* its goals will be achieved (strategy).

Strategy (The *How*)

An organization's strategy outlines *how* it will fulfill its vision and achieve its mission. By understanding their strengths and weaknesses (internal analysis), businesses and ministries can effectively leverage their strengths and improve their weaknesses for their organization's benefit. By conducting an external anal-ysis, businesses and ministries can assess their opportunities and threats to determine which opportu-nities are worth pursuing and which threats need to be avoided or overcome. An organization's internal analysis and external analysis (also known as a "SWOT Analysis"—**S**trengths, **W**eaknesses, **O**pportunities, **T**hreats) will provide the information needed to create and execute effective strategies.

The Value of Vision

All successful organizations have a vision. They know why they exist and what they want to become. According to the book, *Developing Business Strategies*, by David Aaker, through having the right vision, businesses are able to accomplish three primary objectives:

1. Provide clarity on the strategic paths that an organization chooses to take.
2. Create core competencies that produce the needed competitive advantages.
3. Inspire the internal and external stakeholders within the company with a higher purpose to the business, beyond just maximizing shareholder wealth.[4]

In an interview with Henry Kaestner, Co-founder and Executive Chairman of Bandwidth, Mr. Kaestner communicated the following in regards to the value of this principle in his business:

Bandwidth was created with a vision to change the landscape of the telecom industry. Anyone can say that they want to change the telecom industry. However, the question then becomes what do you do and how do you do it? Bandwidth has created a team of over 400 professionals with skillsets ranging from engineers, software coders, wireless

---

[4] David Aaker, *Developing Business Strategies* (Canada: John Wiley & Sons, Inc., 2001, Sixth Edition), 26-28.

experts, and more. We have identified various market segments where we focus our efforts and have made the investments necessary in order to build a team that provides our customers superior, unique value. An organization's vision, mission, and strategy are crucial for it to be able to define purpose, create objectives, and develop strategies to achieve its goals.

Similar to a business's vision, a ministry's vision will enable it to accomplish at least three primary objectives:

1. Provide clarity on strategic paths.
2. Create unique capabilities that enable it to serve others in distinctive ways.
3. Inspire those internal and external to the organization with a purpose that has eternal significance.

International Leadership Institute (ILI) is a global ministry that understands the importance of having vision. In the statement below, Kyle Philips, USA Director of ILI, expresses the importance of vision to his ministry:

The International Leadership Institute clearly articulates its vision through our training, resources, and social media networks. ILI exists "to change history by accelerating the spread of the Gospel through leaders of leaders empowered by the Holy Spirit." ILI recognizes that empowered Christian leaders give concrete, real world expression to God's mission to reach the lost and advance His kingdom. Throughout the Bible and church history, we see God using normal people who come alive when they discover His vision for their lives, cultivate an intimate relationship with Him, and live out His passion for the lost.

The key to ILI's leadership development model goes beyond coaching and personal competencies. Making "disciple-making disciples" is the secret to its expansion around the world. Multiplying others to become leaders, who in turn equip others, drives a deeper integration of ILI's eight core values in the lives of leaders who reproduce themselves. Clearly expressing the goal of "leaders equipping leaders" keeps the global ILI community energized around the essential task of raising up leaders who are empowered to transform others.

As leaders identify their own vision and then begin organizing themselves and their faithful communities around that vision, their world changes. David Thagana is one such leader. Through his vision and ILI training, he has seen over 60,000 leaders throughout East Africa equipped and unleashed to reach out to orphans, slum dwellers, and unreached people groups.

Every Christian ministry should have a clearly defined vision and invest in what it takes to bring it to fruition.

When an organization's vision, mission, and execution strategy work in synchrony, the benefits are experienced by everyone it interacts with. Like business professionals, ministry leaders should place high importance on understanding *why* their ministry exists, *what* they want to do, and *how* they plan to do it. A ministry *with* vision:

1. Creates a team with shared beliefs and values.
2. Knows *why* it exists, what it wants to become, and what it wants to ultimately achieve.
3. Understands what assets it needs, such as people, technology, partnerships, facilities, or funds.
4. Understands what competencies it needs, such as organizational skills, in-depth knowledge of the Bible, teaching, leadership, finance and accounting, project management, and more.
5. Understands what processes need to be defined and documented so that task implementation is accomplished at consistent levels of high quality.

Equally as important to a ministry *with* vision, a ministry *without* vision:

1. Lacks clarity about who its service audience is and what it is striving to do for them.
2. Is unclear on how much financial support is needed, where to find the right financial partners, or how to attract the right financial partners to help fund the ministry.
3. Fails to attract the necessary volunteers, strategic partners, and staff members to help achieve its goals.
4. Is unclear on how to leverage its strengths and improve its weaknesses.
5. Cannot properly identify opportunities or threats that may steer the direction of the ministry in one way or another.

Similar to a business, a ministry's vision, mission, and execution strategy make all the difference in what it can achieve within each of its Five Key Contexts.

Service Audience

Business Logic. Some businesses create sales strategies based on *what* they provide their customers, such as unique products or services that are superior to the competition. Other businesses create sales strategies based on *how* they do what they do, showing customers that they will receive greater value based on the business's unique processes or methodologies. In most cases, these are effective strategies. Many customers, however, want to understand more than just what a business does or how it does it. They want to associate themselves with a business that has a purpose beyond solely making a profit. Businesses with a clear vision and purpose for their existence can create emotional connections with their customers—connections that help drive sales and create long-term relationships.

Ministry Logic. Christian ministries have various attributes that enable them to create connections with their service audience as well—connections that can lead to long-term relationships. A ministry's beliefs, values, vision, mission, and strategy are the predominate attributes that determine what its service audience thinks and feels about the ministry. These attributes help create emotional, intellectual, and spiritual connections that can serve as the foundation of new or long-term relationships.

- <u>Beliefs</u> – A ministry's beliefs express what it believes about Jesus and the Bible, which can instantly create spiritual connections with its service audience.
- <u>Values</u> – A ministry's values communicate what drives its decision-making, which can create emotional connections with its service audience, especially if the values are shared.
- <u>Vision</u> – A ministry's vision helps its service audience understand why the ministry exists, which shows the service audience that they are part of a larger, long-term plan to achieve something significant.
- <u>Mission</u> – A ministry's mission describes the impact it is striving to make for the people it serves. This helps the service audience understand how they will benefit from being in a relationship with the ministry.
- <u>Strategy</u> – A ministry's strategy shows the methodology or process behind how it plans to fulfill its vision and achieve its mission. This creates confidence in the minds of the service audience that the ministry can execute the plans it creates.

Financial Partners

Business Logic. Investors want to be sure that they invest in businesses that have both short and long-term viability. Businesses with a clear vision for why they exist are perceived as more authentic in the minds of investors. Similar to the customer context, most investors want to have a connection with the business they invest into—an emotional connection that makes them excited about being associated with the business. A clear, achievable, and inspiring vision can create this kind of connection. Additionally, investors want to be sure that a business knows the difference it wants to make for its customers (mission) and how it intends to do it (strategy). Clearly presenting a vision, mission, and strategy increases the attractiveness, credibility, and authenticity of the business in the mind of an investor who wants to be a part of something that will make positive short and long-term impacts.

Ministry Logic. Financial partners generally align with ministries that share their own beliefs and values. A ministry that clearly communicates its beliefs and values provides financial partners clarity on who the ministry is and what drives its decision-making. Additionally, financial partners want to invest in ministries with plans for the future and strategies to bring the plans to fruition. The following example illustrates how a new ministry seeking funds to serve the lost in Asia can create connections with the financial partners from whom it is seeking donations:

- <u>Beliefs</u> – Jesus is the Son of God and the only way to enter Heaven is through a personal relationship with Him.
  - o Financial partners have no doubt where this ministry stands on their belief in Jesus, which removes any anxiety about investing in a ministry that does not share their own beliefs.

- <u>Values</u> – (1) Service: serving the poor, (2) Outreach: reaching the lost, and (3) Love: loving the sinner.
  - o Financial partners will know what values help drive the ministry's decision-making.
- <u>Vision</u> – To respond to the Gospel by leading 50 million people to Jesus by 2050.
  - o Financial partners understand why the ministry exists and what its ultimate goal is.
- <u>Mission</u> – To equip and empower local Christians in Asia to evangelize and provide on-the-ground discipleship to new believers.
  - o Financial partners recognize what the ministry is striving to do and the impacts it desires to make.
- <u>Strategy</u> – Partner with local churches and international Christian organizations to identify, equip, and empower local Christians in Asia to preach the Gospel, plant churches, and create sustainable discipleship.
  - o Financial partners see how the ministry plans to fulfill its vision and achieve its mission (understanding that there are many details packed into this strategy).

Volunteers

Business Logic. A business's vision, mission, and strategy help clarify the quantity and types of suppliers needed to help the business achieve its goals. Suppliers are third-party organizations that sell unique products or services designed to help businesses execute their strategies. A business's vision and mission can help motivate suppliers to want to be a part of what the business is doing, which makes developing strategic supplier relationships a much more efficient and effective process.

Ministry Logic. Volunteers *supply* ministries with labor and expertise at no cost to help ministries scale their operations and execute their strategies. Your ministry's beliefs, values, vision, and mission may be what initially attracts volunteers to sacrifice their time to help your ministry serve others. Once volunteers have expressed an interest in serving, it is critical that they understand how your ministry intends to positively impact other people (your strategies). This will ensure that volunteers are clear on why your ministry needs them, what their roles are, and how they will help your ministry achieve its goals.

Strategic Partners

Business Logic. In a "joint-venture" strategic partnership, two businesses determine that they will each benefit from creating a new business entity focused on achieving shared goals. For a joint-venture to even be possible, each business must have a clear understanding of the other in terms of their strengths and weaknesses and how collaboration together can benefit each organization in various ways. Once a partnership is formed, the vision, mission, and execution strategy of the venture must be agreed upon and clearly understood so that both organizations work as one to fulfill a shared purpose.

Ministry Logic. If two ministries see value in forming a strategic partnership, their own respective beliefs, values, vision, and mission will attract one another in the initial stages. The two ministries might make a decision to form an alliance to fulfill a shared purpose that can only be accomplished by working together. If the alliance creates an entirely new ministry, the new entity will be based on common beliefs and values and will create a vision, mission, and execution strategy of its own.

Partners International is a ministry that advances God's Kingdom through the platform of strategic partnerships. In speaking about his ministry, the President and CEO of Partners International, Larry Andrews, said the following words:

> *Our vision is the fulfillment of the Great Commission as commanded by Jesus—to go and make disciples of all of the nations—that is every tongue, every tribe, and every nation. Our mission is to build the church in the least reached places. We do this by connecting the global Christian community to bring the Gospel of Jesus Christ specifically to the least reached, least resourced nations on earth. We accomplish this uniquely through Christ-centered, strategic, and trusting partnerships with indigenous ministry organizations who have a vision to advance the Kingdom of God in their nation.*

> *A ministry's vision needs to be a crystal clear and fiercely protected source to ensure that, as an organization, there isn't any unintended mission drift and that every strategy works towards fulfilling the vision and achieving the mission. In our case, we exist to fulfill the Great Commission by bringing the Gospel of Jesus to unreached groups, explicitly through partnerships with local ministry organizations. Our vision and mission are the guardrails for which all our organization's values, principles, strategy, action plans, and metrics are aligned to.*

> *I think the same principles that drive Partners International apply to every organization, but even more so to a faith-based organization. God has a personal calling for every individual, and it is essential that ministries align themselves with people that share a common vision and mission. When aligned in obedience to God, the capacity to which He can use us in the things we are called to is maximized.*

Staff

Business Logic. If a business's staff members have a clear sense of *why* their company exists, *what* it does, and *how* it does it, they will operate with a high-level of confidence. Highly reputable companies with strong employee retention ensure that the top and bottom levels of their organizations share the same understanding of *why* they do *what* they do, and *how* they do it.

Ministry Logic. For any ministry to efficiently and effectively live out the Lord's calling, it must have the right people on board to make its vision a reality, its mission possible, and its strategy executable. A ministry's beliefs, values, vision, and mission are key elements in attracting and retaining the needed staff to help create and execute its strategies. A small group of people with shared goals can do amazing things, especially when God is at the center and their plans are in accordance with His will.

Larry Andrews also discussed the impact of Partners International's vision and mission in regard to his staff members:

> *Ultimately, every employee at Partners International has a set of work objectives that stem from the relationship between our vision, mission, and strategy. Our work objectives create individual action plans and metrics that support our organizational action plans and metrics. It is critical that all of our action plans align with our vision and mission to insure that we are maximizing the efficiency and effectiveness of what the Lord is calling us to do.*

Visualize

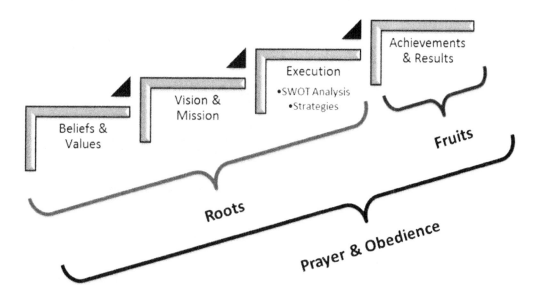

The *Why* Chain

A smart ministry understands the importance of having vision.

- Why?
  - o   Vision creates purpose and provides direction. Creating goals and objectives is only possible if you understand why you are doing something.
- Why?
  - o   If you understand why you are doing something, you will know what impact you are trying to make (mission).

- Why?
  - If you know what impact you are trying to make, you will know who you are trying to impact (service audience).
- Why?
  - If you know who you are trying to impact, you will know who you need in order to help make the impact possible (financial partners, volunteers, strategic partners, and staff).
- Why?
  - If you know who you need, you will know what you need to help make the impact possible (assets, resources, and more).
- Why?
  - If you know what you will need to make the desired impact, you will know how to execute your plans (strategies).

Rhyme *for* Reason

❖ *A ministry with vision*
❖ *Will never go without,*
❖ *A plan to achieve its goals*
❖ *And the mission it has set out.*

❖ *It knows what it will need*
❖ *To honor God and honor man,*
❖ *But a ministry without vision*
❖ *Is like a house on sinking sand.*

Scriptural Application

Bible Verses

John 18:37 – "'You are a king, then!' said Pilate. Jesus answered, 'You say that I am a king. In fact, the reason I was born and came into the world is to testify to the truth. Everyone on the side of truth listens to me.'"

Matthew 28:19-20 – "Therefore go make disciples of all nations, baptizing them in the name of the Father, and of the Son, and of the Holy Spirit, and teaching them to obey everything I have commanded you. And surely I am with you, always, to the end of the age."

Commentary

As Christians, we know that God is a planner and at the essence of planning is vision. When it comes to God and vision, He is the only one that can cast it, knowing full and well what the outcome will be and when it will come to fruition. From that perspective, we cannot relate to Him. Since God is not bound by time, it is interesting to think about His perspective on the plans He sets in motion—He already sees the end and every detail that it takes to get there.

Since creation, God's plan has been to send His Son, Jesus Christ, into the world to restore mankind's relationship to Him. Because of this plan, God's vision for humanity is for all to come to saving faith through a personal relationship with Him. *Why*? Because He loves us. In John 18:37, Jesus briefly delivered a purpose statement for His first coming—to testify to the truth. This purpose is in full support of God's vision, as it is only by believing in the truth that a restored, personal relationship with God is possible.

In Matthew 28:19-20, Jesus invites us to participate in the fulfillment of God's vision for humanity. God has invited us to share in the fulfillment of His vision, participate in the purpose of why Jesus came, and execute His mission through the power of the Holy Spirit. It is quite amazing.

See pages 149-158 for "Action Questions" related to this principle.

CHAPTER 2

Market Intelligence

"Any fool can know. The point is to understand." — *Albert Einstein*

When business plans or marketing strategies are created, one of the most important components of the overall plan is defining the market, or in other words, defining who the prospective customers are. A "market analysis" is done so that a realistic expectation can be set in regards to how many customers a business believes it can create and in what period of time it can do so. A primary function of a market analysis is to enable a business to focus on a targeted group of customers within the total market it is pursuing. This same process applies to any ministry when determining the specific group of people (service audience) it desires to serve.

A market analysis generally begins with identifying the "total market." The total market broadly defines the market in a way that outlines information such as:

- For a business, the total quantity of prospective customers that exist.
- For a ministry, the total quantity of service audience members that exist.

- For a business, where the customers are located.
- For a ministry, where the service audience members are located.

- For a business, how much money customers are already spending on the same (or a similar product or service) that the business offers.
- For a ministry, the fixed and variable costs required to efficiently and effectively serve those in need, in addition to understanding how the service audience is already being served by other ministries.

- For a business, understanding the problems its customers face and how to appropriately solve them.
- For a ministry, understanding the problems its service audience members face and how to appropriately solve them.

If a business's total market is too large to pursue all at once, it is segmented down based on different variables to create a "target market." As a business example, if a total market has 1,000,000 prospective customers, a business may define its optimal target market as only being 10% of the total market. One might ask, "But what about the other 90%?" Yes, narrowing down a total market to a target market will exclude 900,000 prospective customers. However, the remaining 100,000 prospective customers will fit the business's customer profile in a better way than the total market, which will create the highest probability of sales being made.

Most businesses prefer to focus their efforts on a smaller market, raising their probability of success, rather than stretching themselves too thin by pursuing an immense market where there is not enough focus of time, talent, and resources. A smart ministry operates with the same mindset by segmenting a total market into a smaller, targeted service audience, creating more focus and maximizing the positive impacts that can be made. Even within a target market, an experienced business knows it cannot expect to convert every prospective customer into a paying customer. Within a target service audience, a smart ministry understands that it will not have the opportunity to serve every person it seeks to serve.

The final step in market segmentation is estimating what businesses call a "projected capture." This helps businesses realistically estimate how many prospective customers they believe they can convert into paying customers within a specific window of time. A more suitable term for ministries is "projected outreach," which estimates how many people they will have the opportunity to serve within a designated time frame. In no way does this approach attempt to put God in a box or limit what He can do in regards to service and outreach. It is simply a practical way to plan and create strategies, knowing that the Lord can make adjustments in any way He sees fit.

The following is an example of how this principle was used during my time at SPS:

> *SPS worked with many different types of customers across numerous industries including retail, banking, advanced technologies, government, and more. While all of our customers needed "IT solutions," the actual solutions we provided varied based on the market's requirements. For SPS to be relevant and attractive to our customers, we had to understand the following:*
>
> - *Which customers were the "low hanging fruit"—the customers we thought were the quickest and easiest for us to establish relationships with. This process helped us segment large groups of prospective customers down to smaller groups so that our sales efforts were focused in areas where we believed we had the highest probability of success.*
> - *The physical location of our customer's sites. This information helped us determine how fast and cost-effectively we could serve them.*
> - *How price sensitive our targeted customers were, as this impacted the types of solutions we offered.*

- *Our customer's regulatory requirements. In government business, for example, we had to ensure that our field technicians had specific clearances and certifications to even be allowed on site at certain locations.*
- *How the customer's purchasing department was organized so that we could understand who the "decision makers" and "influencers" were during the sales process.*

Understanding how to segment a total market and estimating the amount of business we could generate within a target market was critical in the formulation of our strategies. To ensure that our strategies were sound, we learned as much as possible about our target markets. We spoke with customers to ensure we understood their needs so that our solutions were valuable to them. We spoke with third-party business partners who had more experience in a target market than we did, and leveraged their experience to help us manage risks. We also subscribed to various industry reports in order to help us better understand the emerging trends and opportunities that existed in the markets we were competing in. Collectively, this information helped us define our target markets and serve them with excellence.

Just as businesses define their target markets by segmenting customers from a larger group (total market), ministries can do the same in regards to how they segment a total service audience into a target service audience.

Prison Ministry Example

If a new ministry has a desire to serve prison inmates, it has to determine why it wants to do so, the ultimate goal it wants to achieve, and what impact it wants to make for those who are incarcerated. To begin the launch of the new ministry, its leaders would have to start by assessing the total prison service audience, which would include every prison. If the outreach model was based on meeting face-to-face with inmates, it would be especially critical for the ministry to narrow down the total service audience into a smaller, target service audience. The size of the target service audience would need to match the ministry's current resources, expertise, experience, and bandwidth. The initial service audience segmentation might look something like this:

- Total Service Audience – Every inmate in every prison.
- Geographical Segmentation – Inmates only in California.
- Further Segmentation – Inmates only in Los Angeles.
- Further Segmentation – Male inmates in Los Angeles.
- Further Segmentation – Male inmates only at a specific prison in Los Angeles.

Segmenting the total prison service audience down to a single prison might be the first place to start. However, additional work could be done to create a more specified target service audience of who the ministry aims to initially serve.

Prior to engaging with the targeted prison, the ministry might have to cut through red tape with the California Department of Corrections and understand what regulatory barriers must be overcome in order to initiate outreach efforts. Once the "barriers to entry" are addressed, the ministry might have conversations with staff members at the selected prison to understand how the inmates are segmented. As an example, the ministry may find that there are more than 3,000 inmates at the prison, with groups of inmates classified by their ethnicity, the crime committed, length of sentence, etc. The ministry may find that there are 600 inmates with a sentence of 5 years or less. The ministry may also find that 150 of these 600 inmates are incarcerated for crimes related to drug use. This initial group of 150 may be the target service audience that the ministry decides to focus on.

What started as a global prison ministry opportunity has now been segmented down to a specific state, specific city, specific gender, specific prison, and specific group of inmates.

This new ministry might be tempted to think, "What about all the other inmates in Los Angeles and other areas throughout California? If we only serve this specific group, won't we be missing out on many other outreach opportunities?" It is true that this segmentation strategy eliminates tens of thousands of inmates and potentially tens of thousands of outreach opportunities. However, if the new prison ministry tried to undertake too much too soon, its effectiveness, efficiency, and impact would likely be significantly diminished. By creating a target service audience of only 150 inmates, the ministry could focus all of its efforts on serving that group as best as possible. If successful, it could grow from there.

Does gaining market intelligence stop here? It can—however, going one layer deeper to understand the target service audience can prove to be highly beneficial in ensuring that the greatest impacts are made. Even within this target service audience of 150 inmates, each person will have different experiences, different ways of thinking, different worldviews, and other distinguishing factors. Approaching each person with a generic way to minister to them would likely minimize the positive results that could be achieved. For the new prison ministry to serve this group of men in the most relevant ways possible, it must be quick to listen and slow to speak. This means its leaders must have a sincere desire to learn about each inmate in order to develop trust and understand how to best serve them. One way to do this is by working to understand the following as it relates to the individuals within the target service audience:

- **Perceptions/Beliefs** – What they perceive to be the purpose of life, family, God, etc.
- **Expectations** – What they expect in life from themselves, from God, and from other people.
- **Interpretations of Value** – Understanding what they value.
- **Motivations** – Understanding what motivates them—their children or family, fear of further consequences of their actions, health risks of drug use, etc.

A new ministry certainly will not be able to acquire this type of information on day one. Relationships and trust must be developed with the inmates, and there are many different ways this can be achieved. One method might be partnering with a former inmate (who is now a Christian) that previously struggled with drug abuse. This strategic resource might help the ministry understand the target service audience more clearly and help reduce the time it takes to break down relational barriers that the ministry may face.

After investing time and resources into this targeted audience, the ministry may see trends in the feedback it receives from the inmates. Based on this knowledge, it would then have the opportunity to expand its operations to serve the same target service audience in other prisons. Additionally, the ministry could use this ministry model to serve other service audience segments in the future.

Online Outreach Example

Global Media Outreach (GMO) is a ministry that is taking the Gospel of Jesus Christ to the world. Their unique ministry model utilizes the Internet as well as mobile technology to reach people that may not be reached through conventional, on-the-ground ministry efforts. Even with GMO's efficient and scalable ministry model, they still leverage the value of this principle by creating target service audiences as well as gaining the intelligence needed to effectively serve them. Jordan Stone, Global Catalyst, describes how GMO uses this principle:

> Global Media Outreach (GMO) has a vision to deliver 12.4 billion Gospel presentations, which by God's grace, will result in:
>
> - Multiple Gospel presentations to the anticipated 8.5 billion people who will have both online and mobile access in the coming years.
> - 1.24 billion indicated decisions for Christ.
> - 150 million people engaged with Scripture-intensive discipleship.
> - 50 million people taking first steps as followers of Jesus with Online Missionaries and being connected to a Scripture-based Christian community.
>
> GMO's "total service audience" is the world. Because of that, we have to create smaller and more targeted service audiences that share common traits, which enable our outreach efforts to be as successful as possible. Within each of our target service audiences, our team creates sub-goals that support our vision to ensure all of our outreach efforts work together towards achieving a common purpose.
>
> While everyone in the world shares the same need for Jesus, each person should not be ministered to in the exact same way. Different backgrounds, world-views, experiences, problems, perceptions, religions, and so on mean that ministries like GMO must have a deep understanding of the people we serve. Having an intimate understanding of our service audiences helps guide outreach efforts and strategies to be as impactful as possible.

For example, when we minister to Hindu-background seekers, our outreach approach is different than when we minister to Muslim-background seekers. We have found that an effective way to engage a Hindu-background seeker is by starting with the fact that there is only One True God. This reality is a new paradigm for Hindus because they come from a faith that worships many gods. This engagement strategy creates the opportunity for us to share with them what we mean by "One True God," beginning the process of building trust, establishing a relationship, and being able to share the Gospel. While this strategy is effective in the Hindu context, it is not as effective when we minister to individuals of the Muslim faith. For each of the groups of people we serve, we develop strategies based on market intelligence insights, which enables our engagement with others to be highly meaningful and relevant.

It is essential for Christian ministries to have an acute understanding of the people they intend to serve. This will result in the proper stewardship of the responsibilities and resources God has entrusted to them.

Market intelligence is critical to the success of every ministry's plans and strategies. Understanding your targeted service audience(s) will positively impact your ministry within each of its Five Key Contexts.

Service Audience

Business Logic. There are numerous market factors that help businesses identify a target market as well as its projected capture. General demographic information such as age, gender, ethnicity, or geographical location can help a business begin to define its target markets. However, this information is only a piece of what is needed to gain the necessary intelligence about a group of prospective customers in order to serve them well. Gaining a more intimate understanding of the target market enables businesses to create offers that are optimally relevant to their prospects, which drastically increases the probability of converting prospects to paying customers. Businesses with sufficient market intelligence understand these factors:

1. How many prospective customers fit their target profile.
2. Where to find their targeted customers.
3. How to reach their targeted customers.
4. The average cost of "acquiring" a customer in fixed costs (costs of operating a business) and variables costs (costs of doing business).
5. The "barriers to entry" that need to be overcome in order to serve their targeted customers.
6. What problems they aim to solve for their target customers.
7. What motivates their target customers to make purchases.
8. What perceptions or paradigms govern how their targeted customers think and act.
9. What investments are required to solve their customers' problems so that the solutions are affordable and deliver the right value (cost/benefit ratio).

10. How to create pricing that is both competitive and profitable (revenue & profitability).
11. What their competitors are currently offering to ensure they are *at least* as good as the competition (competitive necessities).
12. What competitive advantages are needed to create more value than the competition (differentiation).

Jim Anthony is the Founder and CEO of Anthony & Company, a real estate firm with operations located in North Carolina. In the following statement, Mr. Anthony highlights the importance of this principle to his business:

> *Originally formed as a brokerage firm in 1956, Anthony & Co. began rapid growth in 1989, capitalizing on business opportunities in industrial, retail, and property development market segments. During the real estate crash from 1989 to 1993, Anthony & Co. turned uncertain circumstances into opportunity by investing in under-performing properties that could be revitalized to create future value for tenants, property owners, and investors. By 2006, we had over $250 million worth of real estate assets under management, including over 1,500 apartments and over 1 million square feet of retail space.*
>
> *Since our company's founding, we have placed heavy emphasis on properly analyzing markets before making any decisions related to investments in land development, property development, and other real estate assets. It is a standard protocol for our team to assess our target market's geographical location, consumer and business population, income levels, price thresholds, competitive offerings, expected benefits, and other factors, to determine how we can deliver maximum value for our clients and business partners. The results that our business continues to produce are directly linked to the level in which we understand the markets we serve. Any organization, business or ministry, should place high value on this principle as it fosters intelligent and confident decision making, which is essential for every organization's success.*

An intimate understanding of a business's target market will enable it to make decisions that carry the least risk and greatest chance of reward. This level of market intelligence will also enable any business to create a key element of its marketing strategy, referred to as a "brand promise," which according to the book, *Brand Aid*, is a "relevant, compelling, and differentiated benefit to the targeted customer"[5]—something every business should have in order to effectively compete.

Ministry Logic. Similar to businesses, Christian ministries should strive to understand the following information as it relates to their target service audience(s) in order to serve them as efficiently and effectively as possible:

---

[5]   Brad VanAuken, *Brand Aid* (New York City: American Management Association, 2003), 38.

1. The quantity of people that make up their total service audience and how to segment it down to create targeted service audience(s).
2. Where the people within the target service audience are located.
3. What other ministries are already doing to serve the target service audience. This intelligence may create a niche that the ministry can serve in a new or better way.
4. The most efficient and effective methods of initiating outreach. This includes understanding various "barriers to entry" that need to be overcome.
5. What should be done to ensure that the target service audience views the ministry as trustworthy and credible.
6. The target service audience's perceptions and beliefs about God, Christians, life, etc.
7. What the target service audience expects *from* God, other people, themselves, etc.
8. The needs of the target service audience (physical and spiritual).
9. What the target service audience values (what is important to them).
10. What motivates the target service audience to seek out solutions to their problems.
11. The average costs of serving a person or group within the target service audience over a select period of time—fixed costs (costs of operating a ministry) and variables costs (costs of outreach).

Acquiring the information above comes in two primary ways. The first way is simply through experience. This route can take time—learning comes from doing, making mistakes, and continuously improving. The second way is through learning from others. One method to accomplish this is by selecting a person or small group of people within the target service audience and learning from them by asking questions, listening to their feedback, and seeing the world from their point of view. This valuable perspective can help ministries save time, enable more strategic planning, and reduce the quantity of assumptions that might lead to avoidable mistakes.

One of the practical reasons why The JESUS Film Project has successfully taken the Gospel to every country in the world is because of the processes they have in place related to market intelligence. The following is a statement provided by Josh Newell, Director of Marketing and Communications for The JESUS Film Project:

> *Since 1979, The JESUS Film Project has taken the Gospel to every country in the world through the platform of film and media. Our goal is to reach every nation, tribe, people, and tongue, to help them see and hear the story of Jesus in a language they can understand. One of the core principles that is at the center of who we are as a ministry is acquiring the intelligence we need to effectively reach every person and people group in the world. Given that "the world" is our service audience, we must be strategic in how we serve through segmenting the total population down to target service audiences. This market segmentation enables our outreach efforts to be as precise, intimate, and impactful as possible.*

Before directly or indirectly taking our media resources into a targeted area, our ministry and strategic partners have a checklist of information that is essential to understand before proceeding. To name a few of these items, (1) We need to determine how large the targeted people group is in quantity of men, woman, and children. This helps us determine the types of media resources we need to make available, costs that will be associated with the outreach effort, and the type and size of the outreach team needed in the event on-the-ground personnel is required. (2) We seek to understand the spiritual beliefs or lack thereof that exist among the people group. This information enables us to be empathetic towards the service audience (by seeing the world through their eyes) in addition to helping us prepare for various responses, questions, or objections they may have after viewing the films. (3) We seek to understand the languages that are spoken amongst the people group. This is an essential part of our ministry model so that we can translate the messages in our films to the native tongue(s). (4) We seek to partner with organizations that have experience with the people group and/or that have served them in some capacity in the past. This helps our process of establishing relationships, creating opportunities to share the Gospel, and creating sustainable discipleship.

Market intelligence enables our ministry to minimize assumptions so that when we create plans and execute them, we are doing so as wisely as possible. Every Christian ministry should focus on understanding the people they serve so that the most effective and efficient outreach can be done.

Financial Partners

Business Logic. A business that understands the dynamics of its target market(s) has a much higher probability of securing investments to help it grow. From an investor's perspective, one of the key areas of analyzing any investment is determining whether the business understands why its solutions are superior to what the competition is already offering. Additionally, investors want to understand what market barriers the business must overcome in order to create sales opportunities that will produce profitable revenue. If a business can show investors that it understands its targeted customers, that there is large sales potential, and that its solutions are better than what is currently being offered, the business will be in a stronger position to obtain investments.

Ministry Logic. Likewise, the more a ministry knows about its service audience and how to best serve them, the higher the probability that its financial partners will be interested to invest. This information includes some or all of the market intelligence factors we have discussed. However, sometimes having in-depth market intelligence before outreach efforts begin is not possible. In this case, a ministry can still utilize the value of market intelligence as it relates to financial partners. This can be accomplished by ensuring that the ministry's financial partners understand the information it plans to gather and how the information will be used once outreach begins. If a ministry is clear on what information is needed to make the greatest impact for its service audiences, the higher the probability of financial partners providing funds to help execute its plans.

Volunteers

Business Logic. When a business understands the dynamics of its markets, it gains clarity on the types of suppliers needed in order to create the best solutions for its targeted customers. If a business does not understand its customers' buying motivations, desired benefits, perceptions, interpretations of value, and more, it runs the risk of partnering with the wrong suppliers. Utilizing the wrong suppliers can negatively impact the offers and solutions the business provides for its customers. Market intelligence will enable the business to select the types of suppliers it needs to be most successful.

Ministry Logic. When a ministry properly understands its target service audience, this awareness brings clarity to the types of volunteers needed to help scale and deliver effective outreach. This enables the ministry to match the appropriate volunteers with specific tasks and responsibilities based on the volunteer's past experiences, expertise, or passions. Furthermore, volunteers will be better prepared to serve others when they understand who they are serving and how they need to serve them.

Strategic Partners

Business Logic. A business's market intelligence may force it to seek out a strategic alliance with another organization to create the necessary competitive advantages to effectively serve its targeted customers. By forming an alliance with the right strategic partner, the business will be able to overcome previous market barriers by offering unique solutions that customers cannot get elsewhere.

Ministry Logic. If a ministry desires to create a strategic partnership with another ministry, one of the best ways to initiate the partnership is by having significant knowledge of its target service audience. This will create confidence in the mind of the potential partner that, in forming a strategic partnership, it will be able to serve the intended audience(s) in ways that achieve the greatest results. Additionally, if two ministries recognize a service audience need, but are unable to appropriately address it on their own, combining different areas of market intelligence can create the perfect formula to benefit all parties. By working together, they can maximize the positive impacts their strategic partnership can create for others.

Staff

Business Logic. A business's staff can be compared to a processing machine that takes raw material and turns it into finished goods. Raw data from the market is acquired in the form of market intelligence. It is then examined, filtered, organized, and translated into strategic marketing messages, sales strategies, and other strategies that enable the business to benefit in numerous ways. There are market research reports that can be purchased, as well as consultants that can help a business increase its market knowledge—however, the business's staff is ultimately responsible for understanding the market with enough clarity to generate sales and produce the desired results for their company.

Ministry Logic. As with a business, a ministry's staff is responsible for creating its target service audiences in addition to determining how to best serve them. Understanding the tangible and intangible qualities of the targeted service audience(s) will enable the ministry to serve with optimal efficiency and effectiveness.

Visualize

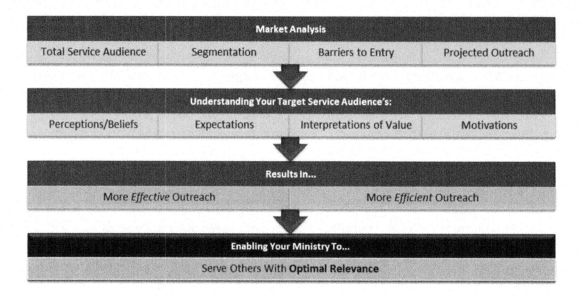

The *Why* Chain

A smart ministry recognizes the importance of properly understanding its service audience(s).

- Why?
  - o Since most ministries cannot be everything to everybody, a total service audience must be segmented into smaller groups of people—target service audiences.
- Why?
  - o Segmented groups of people have a higher probability of sharing common characteristics or attributes, which enables ministries to serve with greater focus. However, even after market segmentation is done, further intelligence should be gathered.
- Why?
  - o Even within smaller, segmented groups, people have varying perceptions, beliefs, expectations, interpretations of value, and motivations. Understanding these attributes creates the opportunity for the most effective and relevant outreach to be done.
- Why?

o   While segmented groups of people may share common characteristics, individuals within each group do not need to be served in the exact same way. Ministries should have "standard outreach procedures" while having the flexibility to customize their approach when required.

Rhyme *for* Reason

❖   *Understanding who you serve,*
❖   *Beyond gender, race, or age,*
❖   *Will make your outreach efforts relevant*
❖   *To anyone's context, life, or stage.*

❖   *Understanding how people think,*
❖   *What they expect and what they believe,*
❖   *Enables solutions to be presented*
❖   *That better serve those who are in need.*

Scriptural Application

Bible Verses

Mark 2:17 – "On hearing this, Jesus said to them, 'It is not the healthy who need a doctor, but the sick. I have not come to call the righteous, but sinners.'"

Mark 6:56 – "And wherever he went—into villages, towns or countryside—they placed the sick in the marketplaces. They begged him to let them touch even the edge of his cloak, and all who touched it were healed."

Commentary

Aside from the 40 days in the wilderness and when He secluded Himself to pray, Jesus was always around people and He understood the settings that He lived and ministered in. As seen in the verses above, Jesus essentially segmented the population in the villages, cities, or countryside into two distinct categories: (1) the "righteous" or those that were "well" and didn't see their need for Jesus and (2) the sinners, the poor in spirit, or those that were sick. Although all people are sinners and salvation is offered to everyone, this "market segmentation" portrays the various ways that Jesus interacted with these two different groups of people. As seen in many examples in the Bible, Jesus' words and how He ministered were not the exact same for everyone. He knew where people were in their lives, understood their views (whether right or wrong), and used different methods of outreach that were optimally relevant to each individual.

*See pages 159-169 for "Action Questions" related to this principle.

CHAPTER 3

Maximizing Credibility

"Every action or perceived inaction shapes credibility." – Mindy Hall

Being viewed as credible is something that every organization strives to achieve. While credibility can be defined in different ways, *The Smart Ministry* defines credibility as an organization that can be trusted to do what it says it will do by operating with a high sense of integrity. Everything an organization does or doesn't do impacts its credibility. No matter what stage of existence a business or ministry may be in, its credibility is formed, strengthened, damaged, or maintained across every facet of its organization.

James Forrest is the Founder of Forrest Firm, a business that provides legal counsel to corporations and entrepreneurs. When asked about the importance of credibility in his business, Mr. Forrest provided the following response:

> *To be a leading provider of professional legal services, we must have a solid combination of experience and expertise acquired through education and practice. At Forrest Firm, we focus on practice areas relevant to the needs of modern business—services ranging from company formation, contract negotiations, and intellectual property protection, to commercial real estate, mergers and acquisitions, and securities. Our clients trust us to provide solutions that will help them lower their risks and strengthen the effectiveness of their operations.*
>
> *Our team of attorneys pledge to deliver sophisticated counsel and customized solutions to each client, and our follow-through on this commitment has resulted in a large client base rewarded by a consistently rising standard of service to each executive and entrepreneur we advise. Our growing client roster and referral base of investment bankers, accountants, and other professionals has helped build our reputation for delivering smart legal counsel in a responsive manner and at competitive prices. A commitment to being perceived as and experienced as a credible organization has been essential in developing our market reputation. Any business or ministry that desires to achieve its goals should have a stead-fast commitment to maximizing its credibility at the personal and organizational levels.*

In 2014, a report found in the book, *Churchless*, revealed that people with no faith of any kind reject God for three primary reasons—one of them being a "lack of trust in the local church."[6] Being in ministry is about relationships, and a "lack of trust in the local church" speaks to the extreme importance for ministries to understand what it means to be credible at personal and organizational levels. The precursor to any fruitful relationship is each party viewing the other as credible—trustworthy and authentic. When you break down a ministry to its fundamental levels, it exists because of two types of relationships: the human relationship with God and the human relationship with other people. In one's personal relationship with God, His trustworthiness is the cornerstone of the relationship. For a ministry, the trustworthiness of its people determines the quantity and quality of relationships it can create with others.

Southland Christian Church is a ministry that understands the importance of maximizing credibility. Here is a story that was shared with me by Southland's Lead Executive Pastor, Chris Hahn:

> *After our founding in 1956, Southland was known as the voice for morality and biblical truth in our Lexington, KY community. We experienced significant growth from the mid-1990s to the early 2000s, and the speed of our growth temporarily outgrew our capabilities to properly function as a ministry. During this time, we experienced difficulties in the areas of finances, staff, leadership, and more. Through a trying time of nearly seven years, Southland restructured our church operations, appointed new leadership (full-time staff and volunteers), and created a church culture that was centered upon relationships that put trust, integrity, and authenticity first. Through persistence, strategic thinking, prayer, and obedience to God's Word, we have been blessed to develop a reputation where it is common for people in our community to say, "If Southland is involved, you know it's going to be done right with honesty and excellence."*

> *Being a church that people trust is essential to us because of two primary reasons. First, Southland exists to reflect the light and love of Jesus, and if we are not trustworthy, we are communicating to a watching world that Jesus is not trustworthy. Second, we have experienced what it is like to go through difficult times where trusting relationships are not present within our church. Those experiences have given us a unique perspective on the value of trusting relationships that are built upon God's Word. Part of Southland's culture today includes making it a priority to openly communicate the "why" behind major decisions we make so that our members, volunteers, partners, and staff have a clearer understanding of the purpose of our decisions. When mistakes are made, we publically address them in addition to publically communicating the actions that are being taken to bring about resolutions.*

> *Transparency and authenticity creates trust, which is the cornerstone of a Christian ministry's influence. When people trust your motives, words, and actions, it is much more likely*

---

[6]   George Barna and David Kinnaman, *Churchless* (USA: Fedd and Company, Inc. 2014) www.barna.org

that they'll grow to trust the God you represent. Every Christian ministry should dedicate itself to maximizing its credibility and the trust it can develop with others.

Maximizing personal and organizational credibility should be a main focus of every ministry in order to function as best as possible within each of its Five Key Contexts.

Service Audience

Business Logic. In 1973, business management legend, Peter Drucker, said, "The purpose of a business is to create a customer."[7] A business's credibility is what puts it in the position to generate sales from paying customers. Prospective customers have so many different options to choose from, but they naturally gravitate toward businesses or brands they trust the most. Credibility factors that develop trust between a business and a customer vary depending on the business's context, but generally speaking, customers will trust a business if it meets or exceeds their expectations on a consistent basis. The customer's expectations are centered on the value that the business says it can deliver via its product or service. If the business keeps its promises, trust is created. If customer expectations are consistently met, trust is built and the customer becomes loyal to the business's brand. If a business exceeds customer expectations, the customer becomes a spokesperson for the business and willingly shares their positive experiences with others. While any business can give products or services away for free in an attempt to exceed customer expectations, the art of business leadership comes into play when customer expectations are met or exceeded in ways that still enable the business to operate profitably.

In his book, *Flawless Consulting*, author Peter Block says, "Consulting is a relationship based business." He also says, "Consulting cannot be done well without genuine caring for the client."[8] Customers hire business consultants because they trust that the consultant's experience and knowledge will enable them to generate new ideas, solve problems, or achieve faster results at a lower cost than alternative options. This knowledge prompted me to obtain my certification as a Certified Business Consultant (CBC), in 2012.

> *In 2012, I was part of a group that consulted to a famous race team in NASCAR. We were introduced to them through a mutual friend, and there were two primary areas in which they needed our services. First, they needed guidance on raising capital for various initiatives they wanted to pursue. Additionally, they needed guidance on creating more effective strategies in order to increase the quantity of sponsorships for their race cars. After understanding the client's needs, we created a consulting proposal centered on three success factors outlined in the book The McKinsey Engagement—"Being clear about the*

---

[7] Peter Drucker, *Management Tasks, Responsibilities, Practices*. (New York City: Harper and Row, 1973)

[8] Peter Block, *Flawless Consulting* (San Francisco: Pfeiffer, 2011), 299.

result, what the engagement will achieve, and the needed involvement of the client."[9]
Our proposal, in addition to the following credibility factors, helped us win the contract.

1. *We were on-time to every call and meeting, which showed that we respected and valued their time.*
2. *We followed up and followed through on every commitment, which showed that we were reliable.*
3. *We properly set expectations about results, communicating what was realistic and what was not.*
4. *We were confident in our capabilities, which increased the confidence the client had in us.*

Ministry Logic. Just as the purpose of a business is to create customers, one of the core purposes of a ministry is to create service audiences. For a ministry to be sure it is being perceived and experienced as credible, it must understand the credibility factors needed in order to develop trust with the people it serves.

David Johnson, Executive Director of Doulos Partners, provided the following statement, outlining the importance of this principle to his ministry:

> *Numerous ministries and ministry leaders have failed. These missteps have brought wide-spread mistrust and cynicism in our culture. That reality has caused Doulos Partners to be fully aware of the extreme importance for us to be above reproach in every area of our organization. In short, we accomplish this by consistently doing what we say we are going to do!*

> *From our inception, Doulos Partners has developed a laser focus. We know who we are and what God has specifically called us to do. Every decision we make has to line up with that purpose, which makes what we say yes to and no to very obvious. Our only interests are evangelism, discipleship, and church planting. Not clearly communicating our vision, how it is carried out, and the results that are being achieved, would make it difficult for others to evaluate the credibility of our ministry. Because of this, we strive to keep our ministry partners connected by giving them monthly reports from the field on quantities of salvations, churches planted, and providing specific stories and prayer needs from our indigenous leaders.*

> *We realize that trust is essential to those we serve and partner with, so we submit ourselves to three outside organizations that vet us each year. Those organizations are:*

---

[9]   Paul N. Friga, *The McKinsey Engagement* (USA: McGraw-Hill Books, 2009), 119.

Evangelical Council for Financial Accountability, (ECFA) Return on Investment Ministry, (ROI Ministry), and Calvin Edwards & Company.

Our ministries are not ours. They belong to Jesus! He IS truth, authenticity, and trustworthiness. We should never do anything to conduct ourselves in a manner that would give the Lord "a black eye." That should be all the reason we need to be completely forthright in all our dealings.

Financial Partners

Business Logic. Smart investors will not invest in something they don't view as credible. If a business doesn't understand the dynamics of its target markets, doesn't understand its advantages over the competition, has a poorly thought-out business plan, or fails to show the investor the opportunity for a positive ROI, investors will likely pursue other opportunities that will provide them with the confidence needed to invest.

Ministry Logic. There is a level of distrust in today's society that has caused people to fear that nonprofits (including Christian ministries) may use donations inappropriately. There are many stories of televangelists and mega-church pastors living lavish lifestyles off of faithful tithes and offerings that were intended for godly purposes. Because of this stigma (in addition to people's desire to invest in things they trust), it is critical that Christian ministries understand how to create and maintain trusting relationships with their financial partners. Financial partners want to know that the money they contribute is being used to honor God and solve the physical and spiritual problems of those in need. Ministries can create and maintain trust with financial partners by being transparent about:

- Why the funds are needed.
- How the funds will be used.
- Who will be impacted.
- When the impacts will be made.
- The expected results that will be achieved.
- The actual results that are achieved.

Volunteers

Business Logic. All businesses want to work with suppliers that are trustworthy and that consistently deliver upon the expectations of value they create. However, credibility in the supplier relationship is not solely based on the supplier's credibility, but on the business's credibility as well. For a business to create long-term relationships with suppliers, it must also be viewed as trustworthy and credible. Suppliers view a business as credible if it is successful at generating sales, pays bills on time, and is easy to work with when issues arise.

Ministry Logic. A primary reason why volunteers choose to serve in a particular ministry is trust. They trust the ministry's plans and the impacts it is making. Trust is also generated through the volunteers' shared beliefs, values, passions, and positive experiences with the ministry. A ministry establishes credibility with volunteers by ensuring they understand what is expected of them, how to properly fulfill their roles, and the importance of their roles in helping the ministry operate and execute its vision and mission.

Strategic Partners

Business Logic. When two businesses are evaluating whether they want to form a joint-venture or other strategic partnership, they conduct mutual due-diligence to assess each other's business on nearly every level. Simply put, they conduct mutual credibility assessments. There is always potential risk in creating a new business entity with another organization when critical areas like sales, profits, losses, and capabilities are shared. To proactively mitigate the known and unknown risks of a strategic partnership, businesses want to be sure that their potential partner is a credible organization—one they can trust, that operates with integrity, and that will make their own company better by joining together.

Ministry Logic. While strategic partnerships can vary based on certain terms and goals, the root of every strategic partner relationship is trust. Like businesses, ministries enter into strategic partnerships where assets, competencies, capabilities, and private information might be shared. This kind of partnership will not flourish without mutual trust, and each ministry must prove through words and actions that they are trustworthy and credible. If they do, they will each be prepared to work within the purpose of their partnership—sharing risks and rewards, staying mutually informed, properly communicating, and experiencing the joy of being successful together.

Staff

Business Logic. The root of any business's organizational credibility is the personal credibility of those that are operating the business. A business may offer an outstanding product or service, however, if its staff are dishonest or unreliable, the business will ultimately fail. For an organization to maximize its trustworthiness and integrity in the eyes of others, it must be committed to hiring employees that are trustworthy and share its values.

Ministry Logic. For a ministry to develop trust with those it interacts with, it must understand each factor that influences its overall credibility. Think of each credibility factor as a key ingredient towards building a credible, trustworthy organization. Trustworthy staff, an essential credibility factor, will help your ministry be perceived and experienced as trustworthy by others. When trust exists, relationships will flourish. Like any organization, a ministry's culture is heavily influenced by its leaders. If the leaders are trustworthy, they will create standards of trustworthiness that will be met (and sometimes exceeded) by their staff. If a ministry wants to be viewed as credible, everything begins and ends with its people.

Visualize

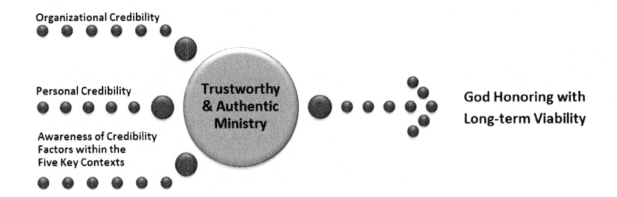

The *Why* Chain

A smart ministry understands the importance of maximizing *personal* credibility.

- Why?
  - If people do not trust you, they will not trust your ministry.
- Why?
  - As an ambassador of your ministry, your role is to develop personal relationships with others that are built upon trust.
- Why?
  - Ministries only grow through personal relationships with people and with God.

A smart ministry understands the importance of maximizing *organizational* credibility.

- Why?
  - If people do not view your ministry as credible, they will not want to be part of it.
- Why?
  - People do not associate with ministries that are untrustworthy.
- Why?
  - People only invest their time and money into things they trust.
- Why?
  - All people desire to achieve a positive return on their investments.
- Why?
  - People want to be associated with things they know will bear fruit—temporally and eternally.

Rhyme *for* Reason

- ❖ *Credibility is the ability*
- ❖ *To show that you're legit.*
- ❖ *The pursuit of credibility*
- ❖ *Is something to never quit.*

- ❖ *If your ministry is credible,*
- ❖ *Relationships will abound,*
- ❖ *That honor God and serve others*
- ❖ *In a way that will astound.*

Scriptural Application

<u>Bible Verses</u>

Matthew 9:6-8 – "'But I want you to know that the Son of Man has authority on earth to forgive sins.' So he said to the paralyzed man, 'Get up, take your mat and go home.' Then the man got up and went home. When the crowd saw this, they were filled with awe; and they praised God, who had given such authority to man."

<u>Commentary</u>

Jesus was fully aware that many of His messages would be hard to believe for some people. Because of this, in Matthew 9:6-8, Jesus demonstrated the importance of credibility within the context of His ministry. Jesus knew that anyone could make a claim, but to tangibly prove what was being said was a different story. In His encounter with the paralyzed man, Jesus told him that his sins were forgiven, which was an audacious and blasphemous statement in the minds of many on-lookers. However, Jesus' credibility and authority were validated when He publicly healed the man of his condition. Jesus knew that this event would increase the faith and trust that people had in Him through the miraculous display of His physical and spiritual authority.

*See pages 170-174 for "Action Questions" related to this principle.

CHAPTER 4

Problem Awareness

"Problems are not stop signs, they are guidelines." — *Robert H. Schuller*

The core purpose of operating a business or ministry is to identify and solve problems. Problems always come in one of two forms: known or unknown. With a known problem, an individual actively seeks out a solution without having to be convinced to do so. With an unknown problem, an individual may not be aware that a solution is needed. This requires organizations to use knowledge, wisdom, and experience to expose the problem so that the need for resolving it is clearly understood.

Usually, a prerequisite to having awareness of a problem is being aware of a solution to that problem. When new solutions become available, they can expose problems that people might otherwise not have known existed. For example, a critical element of a high-tech company's sales strategy is making its customers aware of problems with existing technology devices. The company's new solutions provide a better experience for its customers, thereby making existing technology seem antiquated and riddled with problems by comparison. This continuous process of innovation creates new paradigms that govern the way people think and perceive.

Henry Kaestner, Co-founder and Executive Chairman of Bandwidth, describes this principle as it relates to his business:

> One of the biggest problems in the telecommunications industry has been the speed at which information is transferred. As time progresses, corporations, and individuals are creating higher standards of what they expect from telecom providers—mainly, how fast they can manage, transfer, and receive information. At Bandwidth, we enable our customers to instantly communicate and receive the information they need so that they can focus on their core business.
>
> Bandwidth has spent over 15 years understanding the problems our customers face, and we create solutions that propel them into a faster, more efficient future. Our software solutions, nationwide IP network, and other solutions have been created through our understanding of the problems our customers experience. Every business and ministry needs to have a focus

on understanding the problems they set out to solve. Clarity on what causes problems creates clarity on what solutions to provide.

One of the most important attributes of problem awareness is perspective. For example, look at our planet from 200 miles up on Google Earth, which is close to the distance of the International Space Station to the surface of the Earth. At 200 miles above the Earth's surface, all that can clearly be seen are land colorations—shades of green, brown, blue, and white. At this view, it would be illogical for someone to think they had a clear understanding of Earth's history, its inhabitants, problems, religions, sin, and more. Their understanding would be extremely limited based on their high-level view and perspective. Now start to zoom in closer to the Earth's surface. Things begin to appear that weren't visible before—rivers, lakes, cities, buildings, streets, trees, cars, and people. What appeared to be a simple planet at 200 miles up has become a dynamic, complex place with an innumerable amount of variables. If someone based their understanding of Earth solely on their 200-mile-view, they'd miss so much of what Earth is all about. The 200-mile-view is important, however, because as you zoom in, it becomes clear how everything fits into the bigger picture. Having awareness of problems (200-mile-view), understanding them in more detail, and understanding what causes them (zooming in) are effective ways for any Christian ministry to approach the problems it aims to solve.

At the 200-mile-view, all Christian ministries have an awareness of one or two types of problems they aim to solve: physical (temporal) and spiritual (eternal). As they start to zoom in, however, they discover that they exist to solve *specific* physical and spiritual problems because it is not possible for one ministry to address every need. As they continue to zoom in, the classification of the problems becomes clear, something that Thomas Freese refers to in his book, *Question Based Selling*, as either a "pain point" (a known ailment) or "desire" (a wish or want).[10] To uncover the root cause of each problem, a ministry can utilize "The Five Why's" technique, referred to in this book as "The *Why* Chain". This process of understanding problems at high-levels, as well as in detail, equips a ministry with the knowledge it needs to implement the right solutions.

Kyle Philips, USA Director for International Leadership Institute, describes the primary problems his ministry is tasked with solving:

> *ILI seeks to awaken the slumbering soul to the great mandate the Lord has given the church. By understanding the sub-biblical paradigms that paralyze our culture, leaders working to equip other leaders can speak directly to the systemic issues hindering the sacrificial, outward looking passion the Lord intends for us.*
>
> *In the American context, we have inherited a church culture that, for the most part, has professionalized ministry. We expect the church's vision to come from its pastor and staff while inviting non-professional believers to participate in the vision with their time and money. When someone hears the word "ministry," they usually think "pastor." The great reformation*

---

[10] Thomas A. Freese, *Question Based Selling* (Naperville: Sourcebooks, Inc., 2000), 69.

doctrine of the priesthood of all believers is understood more in abstraction than in reality. Consequently, the vast resources of believers in the USA remain untapped as they serve the vision of others, often half-heartedly. When the people in the pews realize that God has vision for them, they ignite with passion, resources are released, and the Gospel accelerates through the community.

Another problem we address is the consumer lifestyle shaping America. The underlying story giving shape to our hopes and dreams is "getting stuff." Our sense of value and meaning comes out of products we purchase to satisfy desires and provide identity. Marketing works to form our decision making around our subjective experiences, stimulated to serve what the market is offering.

Our churches often conform to that pattern of outreach in seeking to meet felt needs to draw people into its organizations. Too often, the biblical call to die to self and to live for God and others is filtered through our "what's in it for me" consumerism and is lost. In that environment, clear imperatives in Scripture become mere suggestions or advice. Take it or leave it, depending on how they might serve our needs.

ILI has found that our awareness of these problems is a mere starting point. Understanding why they exist and what causes them at macro and micro levels motivates us to work towards solutions that glorify God. Every ministry should clearly understand the problems they desire to solve in order to create plans and implement solutions that honor God and benefit others.

Being aware of problems and understanding the dynamics surrounding them will positively impact every Christian ministry within each of its Five Key Contexts.

Service Audience

Business Logic. When a customer's problems are known, a business is tasked with appropriately responding to the demand the customer has created. Commercial customers will usually issue RFPs (requests for proposals), which are documents outlining their need for a solution. The responding businesses then create proposals outlining their understanding of the customer's needs, solution recommendations, pricing, and reasons why they are superior to the competition. Upon reviewing each proposal, the customer selects the business they believe offers the best solution.

The most successful businesses appropriately respond to a customers' known problems in addition to exposing their unknown problems. If a business seeks to make customers aware of unknown problems, it is *creating customer demand*. Additional time, money, and strategies are needed in order to effectively do this. However, such investments can pay off if the created demand leads customers towards better ways of thinking and operating.

In the chemical world, a form called a MSDS (Material Safety Data Sheet) communicates nearly everything one would need to know about a chemical product. The form includes the identity of the product's manufacturer, the ingredients of the product, the health hazards, the safety hazards, the environmental hazards, and more. Nearly every commercial company that purchases chemicals is required by Health Department inspectors to have MSDS forms available on-site for reference and training purposes. Each MSDS form has various health and safety classifications with ratings from 0 (extremely safe) to 4 (extremely hazardous). If used without caution, products with a 3 or 4 rating can result in permanent blindness, severe skin burns, severe respiratory illness, or even death. Within the markets that eWater focuses on, we compete against chemicals that generally have health and safety ratings ranging from 2 to 4.

In most cases, eWater's customers are not aware of their chemical product ratings for a number of reasons. However, it is our job to ensure that the customer is made aware of such risks when we educate them about the unique attributes of our products. eWater's solutions have MSDS forms as well, but the health and safety ratings are 0 or 1. This difference is paramount, because it means the customer will significantly lower their risk of employee injury or illness, environmental impact, and more. In order for our customers to make a well-informed purchasing decision, it is critical that they are aware of their current risks and that they understand how switching to eWater's solutions will reduce or eliminate those risks.

Ministry Logic. Similar to a business, a ministry's viability is largely dependent upon its awareness and understanding of the problems it aims to solve. For known problems, a ministry must understand *why* the problems exist in order to lead its service audience towards seeking out the right solutions. If the known problem is a "pain point," such as a physical or emotional ailment, the ministry must have the right people, processes, and capabilities in place to provide the necessary solutions.

For a ministry to effectively address unknown problems, more time and investment may be required. Ministries that focus on evangelism are addressing what many consider to be an unknown problem—sin. In most cases, a Christian minister doesn't just walk up to a non-believer, tell them they have a sin problem, that Jesus is the answer, and expect them to be receptive to what they are hearing. To help someone recognize their sin problem and need for Jesus, they must be educated on the credibility of the Bible, who God is, and how Scripture is relevant to them. By sharing the Word in undiluted form, giving personal testimony, and praying for God's intervention, the Holy Spirit can change one's desires and expose the problems only God can solve. When new desires are created—desires that match God's—real change occurs.

Global Media Outreach provides a unique platform for anyone with Internet access to learn more about Jesus. GMO's Internet presence helps those who are seeking purpose and truth to become aware of their personal need for Christ. Michelle Diedrich, Executive Director of GMO, provided the following statement supporting the value of this principle to her ministry:

Global Media Outreach (GMO) is a ministry that exists to share Jesus with seekers and helps them to understand transformational renewal in Christ. Millions of times every day, people search the Internet for hope and are open to spiritual transformation. Many times they are in crisis or aren't even sure what answers they're looking for and can't or won't turn to friends, neighbors, coworkers, or family.

The opportunity for online missions is increasing every day. The use of Internet and mobile technology continues to grow at tremendous rates worldwide, and these platforms are becoming common ground for people that are searching for truth and purpose to their lives. Traditional on-the-ground missions can have formidable costs and access barriers to share Jesus. In response to this, God is using technology to transform our ability to reach beyond geographic, cultural, and religious boundaries to share the Gospel through online ministry. GMO provides the most scalable model of outreach, using technology to reach the millions who are searching for spiritual help. This virtual "Roman Road" takes the Gospel to the world.

Sixty-percent of the world's population (over 4 billion people) live in the 10/40 window, home to Islam, Buddhism, Hinduism, and other religions. These areas are the least likely to have heard the Gospel because of cost, governmental, and geographical access barriers. Having awareness of such problems, GMO's model of online access provides a way for people in these areas to learn about Jesus in their own language, while being ministered to by Online Missionaries at a time when they are most open to hearing the Good News.

Global Media Outreach is helping the lost in our world have instant access to the Gospel and discipleship. Our awareness of people's need for Jesus, barriers with traditional on-the-ground missions, and the contemporary avenues through which spiritual help is being sought out has created a ministry model we believe God will continue to use for years to come. By having a clear understanding of the problems it intends to solve, every Christian ministry will be able to define its purpose and reason for being in a way that resonates with others and brings glory to God.

Financial Partners

Business Logic. When businesses aren't properly capitalized, there isn't enough cash available to successfully execute their vision and mission. Under-capitalization is a known problem. Businesses that find themselves in this scenario seek outside investments from individuals or organizations. While some investors are strictly financial investors with no operational influence in the business they invest in, others are strategic investors. Strategic investors invest money to help with capital needs and also invest their expertise to help the business achieve its goals. For strategic investors to determine if the investment opportunity is a good fit, they must be aware of the problems the business intends to solve within their target markets—both known and unknown. This awareness will help provide investors with additional clarity on why the business exists and what it is striving to do.

Ministry Logic. All ministries share a fundamental problem—the need for money to operate successfully. Most financial partners are aware of this problem, however, they usually are not aware of the specific details surrounding it. Because of this, there is a gap between the ministry's awareness/understanding and the financial partner's awareness/understanding in regard to financial needs. It is the ministry's responsibility to bridge the gap to ensure there is mutual awareness and understanding. Many financial partners will want to be aware of the specific problems the ministry is facing and will want to understand each problem with as much clarity as possible to accurately determine if they can help. If financial partners don't clearly understand how their funds will be used and what benefits will result from their contributions, they will likely take their money elsewhere.

Additionally, financial partners will gain a clearer sense of your ministry's purpose when they understand the problems your ministry solves for its service audience. The better they understand why your ministry exists, the greater the probability of securing financial contributions.

Volunteers

Business Logic. The process of creating a product or service and delivering it to a customer is known as a "supply chain." This includes raw materials, product manufacturing, value-added components, warehousing, packaging, pricing, shipping, and post-sale customer service. Businesses that offer the highest value products and services, generally have the strongest supply chains. Supply chains create an acute awareness of the different areas in which problems can arise, and are designed to proactively solve each problem. A supply chain can include any number of suppliers who are needed to create a finished, customer-ready solution. Businesses with strong supply chains work with suppliers to ensure they understand their role and where their value fits within the entire equation. This creates greater commitment from suppliers to consistently perform as the business needs them to.

Ministry Logic. Ministries can view their volunteer base as a "volunteer chain." Volunteers are critical in a ministry's ability to deliver services and solutions that appropriately solve problems. Any ministry can evaluate its need for volunteers by asking the following question, "Can we accomplish all of our goals solely with the people we have on staff?" If the answer is yes, the goals may not be ambitious enough. The majority of the time, however, the answer is "no," which creates awareness for when, where, and how volunteers are needed—the volunteer chain. While God can do anything through anyone, practically speaking, I believe He uses volunteers as a way to bless ministries, enabling them to grow and succeed without incurring significant costs. Having awareness of your ministry's operational problems by only utilizing staff members, will help create a volunteer chain that benefits your ministry and shows volunteers how much they are needed and valued.

Strategic Partners

Business Logic. The beginning of most strategic partnerships is problem awareness. A business is usually aware of problems it has, and this awareness leads it to seek out a strategic partner in order to solve its problems. Here is an example: Business A has a new energy management product that will help restaurants save money by monitoring and reducing their electrical use. Business A also has a problem. Due to a number of market entry barriers, it is having difficulty making prospective customers aware of this new solution. Business A finds Business O, a prospective strategic partner. Business O currently works with thousands of restaurants by installing and repairing their electrical systems. Business O's current customers are Business A's prospective customers. Business A believes that Business O can help it gain visibility to its target customers since Business O is already serving them. Unknown to Business O, Business A's energy management product can be distributed by Business O, which will create a new revenue opportunity for Business O while simultaneously increasing the value it can offer.

By forming a strategic partnership, Business A's market exposure problem is solved through Business O's market presence. Business A is also able to show Business O that, by joining together, Business O will benefit from a new revenue opportunity (this exposes a need Business O wasn't aware of). The end result? Business A and Business O are able to offer their customers a new energy management solution (exposing a problem restaurants didn't know they had). It's a win-win-win.

Ministry Logic. Christian ministries may determine that the best way to address a problem is by partnering with another organization via a strategic alliance. Having an awareness and clear understanding of the problem is essential to the process of identifying the right partner, in addition to communicating the benefits of partnering together. The key is not to approach a strategic partner with the goal of only solving your own problem. Your ministry must be able to solve a problem your partner has as well, whether it is known or unknown to them at the time of your initial engagement. Additionally, if your ministry and your prospective strategic partner are already serving the same service audience, try to identify a problem the service audience has that can only be solved by partnering together.

Staff

Business Logic. For any business to be successful, its staff must be trained to appropriately respond to known problems, in addition to exposing problems that are not known. Just because a problem is known does not mean it will be properly handled, and just because a problem is unknown does not mean it doesn't exist. Some problems take time to adequately understand and solve, requiring persistence and determination. Staff members that can understand problems in depth, as well as identify problems before others are aware of them, can create sustainable competitive advantages that position their organization for success.

Ministry Logic. As the execution arm of a ministry, staff members must be aware of and understand all of the problems their ministry has set out to solve (physical and spiritual). It is crucial to understand each problem at a high-level (200-mile-view) in order to see how it fits into the big picture. Zooming in enables the problem to be understood in finer detail, which brings clarity to what action needs to be taken. By having the proper understanding of each problem your ministry aims to solve, the quantity of service and partnership opportunities will be maximized.

Visualize

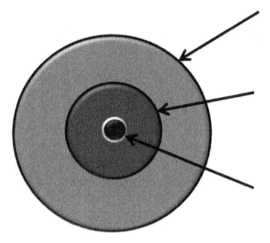

Reverse Bulls-Eye Diagram

MAXIMUM IMPACT

Clear understanding of the problems your ministry solves. Maximizes service and partnership opportunities.

MEDIUM IMPACT

General understanding of the problems your ministry solves. Missed service and partnership opportunities.

MINIMAL IMPACT

Lack of understanding of the problems your ministry solves. Minimizes service and partnership opportunities.

The *Why* Chain

A smart ministry understands the importance of having an awareness and understanding of the problems it aims to solve.

- Why?
  - To adequately understand a problem, it must be understood at macro and micro levels.
- Why?
  - A macro understanding provides a high-level perspective of the problem. A micro understanding exposes the problem's dynamics and causes. Both perspectives are needed.
- Why?
  - A minimal or general understanding of the dynamics of a problem may result in the implementation of faulty solutions that waste time, energy, and money.
- Why?
  - Looking at a problem from different perspectives exposes the problems attributes. This provides clarity and direction on which solution to implement.

Rhyme *for* Reason

- ❖ *Being aware of the problems you solve*
- ❖ *At the 200-mile-view,*

- ❖ *And understanding them at their depths*
- ❖ *Is what you should always strive to do.*

- ❖ *If the problem is only physical*
- ❖ *Or if it's just spiritually related,*
- ❖ *Understanding why it exists*
- ❖ *Ensures the right solution will be created.*

Scriptural Application

Bible Verses

John 3:3-4 – "Jesus replied, 'Very truly I tell you, no one can see the kingdom of God unless they are born again.' 'How can someone be born when they are old?' Nicodemus asked. 'Surely they cannot enter a second time into their mother's womb to be born!'"

Commentary

During Jesus' public ministry, one way He consistently got the attention of on-lookers, followers, and skeptics was by addressing known problems that people had, whether it be hunger, thirst, or physical ailments. In John 3, Jesus made Nicodemus aware of an *unknown* problem he had. In order to see the Kingdom of God, Nicodemus had to be born again, or in other words, His sin had to be forgiven by the only One with the power to forgive sins. We are very similar to Nicodemus in that, when we are presented with information that exposes an unknown problem, our initial reaction can be one of disbelief and confusion. No matter how much we object or put up walls in our ignorance, the truth exposes our needs and problems. Thanks be to God that neither Nicodemus, nor you and I, have to figure out how to solve problems on our own. God is with us and will provide us with wisdom and direction on our journey.

*See pages 175-183 for "Action Questions" related to this principle.

CHAPTER 5

Problem Implications

"Wisdom consists of the anticipation of consequences." — Norman Cousins

A problem's implication means that if a problem goes unresolved, then guaranteed or likely negative consequences will result. In order to adequately understand the dynamics of a problem, you must also understand the problem's implications. Think about a recent problem you've experienced. What would or could have happened if you didn't resolve it? Whatever the circumstance was, knowing the problem's implications was probably a driving force that spurred you to seek out a solution. Understanding the implications of the problems you face is equally important as understanding the problems themselves.

"If-then" statements can be very useful in understanding a problem's implications. "If" describes the problem and "then" describes the implication. Here are a few examples in business and ministry:

1. If a business doesn't adequately understand the dynamics of its target market(s), then it will create solutions that fail to satisfy the market's needs.
2. If a ministry fails to define its vision and mission, then it risks operating without a clear sense of purpose and direction.
3. If a business operates without a website, then making customers aware of its products or services will be difficult.
4. If a ministry fails to understand the causes of its service audience's problems, then it will not be equipped with the knowledge to create lasting solutions.
5. If a business prices its products too low, then it may fail to generate enough profits to cover operating expenses.
6. If a ministry is untrustworthy, then it will fail to create sustainable relationships.

Problem implications can be (and should be) motivating factors that spur people to take action. Taking action doesn't guarantee the desired results will be achieved, but by fully understanding the dynamics of a problem, you will be better positioned to implement the best solution.

James Forrest, Founder of Forrest Firm recognizes the value of this principle as it pertains to practicing business law:

Business law, by nature, is about risk management, and business attorneys must be especially keen at seeing the bigger picture and thinking several steps ahead for their clients. At Forrest Firm, we must understand the scope of our clients' challenges, their potential responses to these challenges, and the potential outcomes of their decisions. Furthermore, we must communicate our understanding of their challenges, along with our best advice for mitigating risks and achieving their business goals in ways that they, too, can understand and carry forward successfully. Informed of the best options at their disposal—options that strike the proper balance between risk management and business development—Forrest Firm's clients are empowered to make the best decisions for their organization.

Every organization should leverage the value of understanding and communicating the implications of the problems it solves. This principle alone develops trust among stakeholders, enabling all parties to reach the most effective solution.

Christian ministries are similar to businesses in regard to their need for understanding problem implications across a variety of contexts. Having a 200-mile-view helps frame the problem from a high-level perspective, while zooming in helps create more clarity around the problem's attributes and cause(s). A critical piece to understanding a problem as a result of the zoomed in perspective is understanding the problem's implications. Sometimes it is difficult to accept the implications of a specific problem, but ministries must be able to operate with what author Jim Collins calls, *"the brutal facts of reality."*[11] While a problem's implications can sometimes have unsettling realities (such as the implications of not placing one's faith in Christ), ministries must face them head-on in order to make (and help others make) the best decisions possible.

Understanding a problem's implications can and will yield numerous benefits within the Five Key Contexts of any ministry.

Service Audience

Business Logic. There seems to be a general perception that sales people are sleazy, manipulative, and will say anything to close a deal. While there are manipulative sales people out there, informing a prospective customer about the implications they will or might experience if they do not seek out a solution, doesn't have to come across as manipulative. It really comes down to how the message is delivered. Good sales people are empathetic towards their customer's problems, and in many cases, they understand the problem better than the customer. For sales people to effectively communicate the implications of a problem without being perceived as manipulative, they must stick to facts or reasonable assumptions about what will or might occur if a solution is not implemented.

---

[11] Jim Collins, *Good to Great* (New York City: Harper-Collins Publishers, 2001), 69.

If sales people can reference factual implications about a customer's problem, they might share stories of past customers they've served or reference studies/tests showing empirical outcomes of what will happen if the problem goes unsolved. If factual information is not available, they will have to rely upon their knowledge of the problem's implications in order to help their customer make the best decision.

Below is an example of how eWater Advantage uses factual information to highlight a problem's implications:

> *Factually speaking, engineered water is superior to chemicals from health, safety, and environmental perspectives. These are strong selling points because they aren't personal opinion but are backed by empirical science.*

> *Another key attribute that distinguishes engineered water from chemicals is how effective it is at killing germs—the degree in which it kills microorganisms as well as the speed in which it kills them.*

> *Engineered water has been proven to be 80 times more powerful at killing bacteria and microorganisms than chemical products. Some of eWater's systems have third-party test results showing that our solution kills microorganisms such as E.coli in 15 seconds, at a 99.99999% kill rate. That's a "Log 7" kill, meaning that only 1 cell of the microorganism remains alive after 15 seconds of contact time with the engineered water.*

> *Educating our customers on why engineered water is superior to conventional chemicals involves informing them of the implications of chemical use: health, safety, environmental, and product efficacy implications. In most cases, once they become aware of this infor-mation, they are excited to know there is a better way.*

*Ministry Logic. **If*** your ministry fails to properly understand your service audience's problems, ***then*** the quantity of outreach opportunities and the quality of service provided will be diminished. One of the best ways to maximize the quantity of outreach opportunities and the quality of service, is to fully under-stand the implications of the problems your ministry solves. The *quantity* of outreach opportunities are maximized because you are able to inform your service audience of the negative consequences that will or might occur if a solution is not implemented. This type of wisdom leads the service audience to have more trust in your ministry. The *quality* of service is maximized for the same reasons, because the best solution can only be provided through an adequate understanding of the problem.

Jonathan Wiles, VP for Program Excellence with Living Water International, describes the importance of understanding this principle as it relates to the physical and spiritual problems that his ministry addresses:

> *On the surface, the physical problems Living Water International addresses seem straight-forward—unsafe water, inadequate sanitation, and insufficient hygiene. The implications*

these problems have on people's lives, however, are extensive. Our ministry also exists to help fulfill the Great Commission by bringing the Gospel of Jesus Christ to the near 2.8 billion people who have never heard of or experienced it.[12] The implications of this problem are eternal. In order to effectively serve the masses that don't have access to clean water and have never heard the Gospel, we dedicate ourselves to understanding these problems as deeply as possible so that we can implement sustainable solutions.

*Unsafe drinking water, inadequate sanitation, and insufficient hygiene leads to 840,000 deaths per year.[13] Poor **w**ater **a**ccess, **s**anitation, and **h**ygiene (WASH) causes 50% of the world's under-nutrition,[14] and people suffering from WASH-related disease occupy half the hospital beds in the world. This health issue is also a root cause of other economic, educational, and social problems that carry significant implications. When water is far from home, 80% of the burden falls on women and children—many of whom walk three to five miles to fetch water multiple times per day. Every year, this costs children 443 million school days and wastes 40 billion hours of labor in Sub-Saharan Africa alone.[15] There's clearly more to this problem than can be seen at first glance.*

It's also important for us to work the problem the other direction, toward its own root causes. As followers of Jesus, we believe that all brokenness in the world—physical and spiritual—is caused by broken relationships between people, with God, and with the Earth we steward. If we don't recognize that there is a constellation of inter-related physical and spiritual problems, we'll never get beyond treating symptoms.

To adequately understand a problem, you must understand its implications. Every Christian ministry should seek to understand the implications of the problems it addresses in order to create lasting, effective, and relevant solutions.

Understanding the implications of not having a personal relationship with Jesus is one of the key drivers that motivates David Johnson, Executive Director of Doulos Partners, and his team to execute their mission on a global scale:

The problem that we exist to solve is the "lostness" of the world. We clearly state the reason we exist, which is to reach the maximum number of people in the shortest amount

---

[12] *Operation World*, 7th Edition (2010), p. 25: http://www.operationworld.org

[13] World Health Organization Fact Sheet #391, July 2014: www.who.int/mediacentre/factsheets/fs391/en

[14] WHO (2008), "Safer water, better health: costs, benefits and sustainability of interventions to protect and promote health" http://whqlibdoc.who.int/publications/2008/9789241596435_eng.pdf

[15] UNDP Human Development Report 2006: http://hdr.undp.org/sites/default/files/reports/267/hdr06-complete.pdf

of time in the most cost effective way. If we are not solving that problem, then we are clearly not carrying out the very reason for our existence. The negative consequences would be catastrophic. Why would someone invest their resources in an organization that is failing to carry out the very reason for its being?

The implications of not being in a personal relationship with Jesus Christ are the very life-blood that drives our ministry. Grasping the reality that we will be measured by the Lord, our partners, and the world, on how we carry out the assignment that we have been given is monumental. When we, as a leadership team, ponder what's next, it is always connected to how can we reach more men, women, boys, and girls with the Gospel, which is the problem that every Christian ministry is called to solve!

The purpose and execution of ministries should always be measured. How else will they and their partners know if they are being successful in carrying out their vision? If ministries are not being fruitful, then they should not be surprised when budgets are not being met, relationships are not being leveraged, and reports from the field are not encouraging. Ministries must stay on target. If not, it is just a matter of time before trouble is at the door!

Financial Partners

Business Logic. Businesses seek financial investments because of a problem they have—under-capitalization (not enough money to do what they need/want to do). The implications of under-capitalization might be the inability to pursue a certain opportunity and/or a lack of funds to sustain operations. These implications can be extremely detrimental, which is why businesses have a high sense of urgency for securing investments.

Problem implications are relevant to investors in another context as well. Investors are always interested in a business's sales strategies, and a key part of any sales strategy is understanding the customer's implications if they choose not to buy what the business is offering. If the customer's implications are significant, the business has a compelling offer and investors will be motivated to invest.

Ministry Logic. **If** your ministry's financial needs are not clearly understood by your financial partners, **then** the chances of raising funds are drastically reduced. Financial partners want to be well-informed on why a ministry needs funding, what the funds will be used for, how the funds will be used, who will be impacted, and what the desired end results are. By proactively answering the first question (why funds are needed), your ministry can successfully address the problem as well as the implications that will or might result if it isn't solved. The key is to ensure that factual information or educated assumptions surrounding the problem implications are clearly communicated, so that financial partners feel confident in making a decision to invest. Educating financial partners in this manner will increase their level of urgency to respond to your ministry and invest their funds.

Volunteers

Business Logic. In the previous chapter, we discussed that businesses create "supply chains" to address the problems that must be solved in order to deliver competitive and attractive offers. Every problem that a supply chain addresses has a set of implications. Here is an example of a supply chain for a custom t-shirt business:

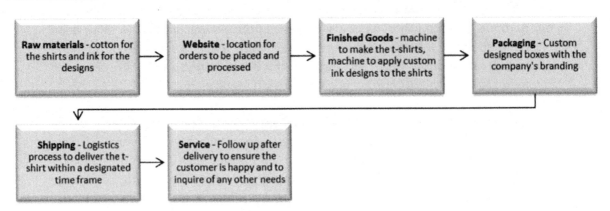

If the business utilizes unreliable cotton or ink suppliers, the implication is failure to consistently produce and sell high quality products. If the website ordering system is faulty or complicated, the implication is lost sales to competitors. If shipping issues are a chronic problem, the implications are unhappy customers and a damaged market reputation. You get the point. For businesses to be competitive, it is crucial that they understand what implications exist if their supply chain malfunctions as well as proactively plan for what to do if/when it does.

Ministry Logic. **If** the appropriate volunteers are not in place, **then** your ministry will fail to operate at its highest levels of efficiency and effectiveness. Volunteers need to understand the implications your ministry will or might face without their commitment and service. This is not to make volunteers feel guilty, but it is meant to motivate them to take action. If volunteers are aware of the potential negative outcomes that will or might result from a lack of volunteer commitments, it can create urgency within them to sacrifice their time. Furthermore, they will approach each service opportunity with a higher sense of purpose, which will produce the best results possible.

Consider creating a "volunteer chain" that outlines general volunteer tasks for your ministry as well as tasks for specific purposes. Document the key areas where volunteers are needed so that everyone clearly understands their role and how it affects others. Understand what will or might occur if a link in the volunteer chain does not function properly. Identify these implications, create training documentation to prevent the implications from occurring, and have back-up plans available in the event they do occur.

Strategic Partners

Business Logic. If a business is faced with a problem that can only be resolved through a strategic partnership, the implication of the problem is clear: the problem will remain unless a strategic partnership is formed. Because strategic partnerships need to be a win-win for both organizations, each entity must be aware of a problem they have in addition to the implications of their problem. This may require one business to expose a need/problem that the other hasn't yet recognized. If the potential of the strategic partnership is known and agreed upon, then the implications of not partnering can serve as the motivation each business needs to partner together.

Ministry Logic. **If** forming a strategic partnership is the best way for your ministry to strengthen an area of weakness or capitalize on a unique service opportunity, **then** you must do what it takes (in alignment with Scripture) to attract the type of strategic partner your ministry needs. Communicating your ministry's vision, mission, and execution strategy can incent a strategic partner to join you in your efforts—this will benefit your organization, theirs, and the people you intend to serve.

Staff

Business Logic. There are operational implications to a business if the wrong people are hired, therefore, a business's human resources department must thoroughly screen potential hires to avoid making a wrong decision. One of the best ways to do this is hiring by values. Many job responsibilities can be taught, so hiring new employees with an emphasis on their values is a better hiring method. Companies that hire by values would rather teach a trustworthy employee how to do a specific job than to hire someone with a long list of accolades who can't be depended upon.

Ministry Logic. **If** you have the right staff members in the wrong roles, **then** your ministry's effectiveness, efficiency, and overall impact will be reduced. Having a good understanding of what will or might occur if the capabilities of your ministry's staff are out-of-place will help your ministry avoid risks and negative outcomes before they occur. The business tactic of hiring by values will most likely be "hiring by beliefs" in a ministry context. However, with the assumption that your staff shares the beliefs that define your ministry, more focus can be placed on the person's experience and other intangible qualities.

Visualize

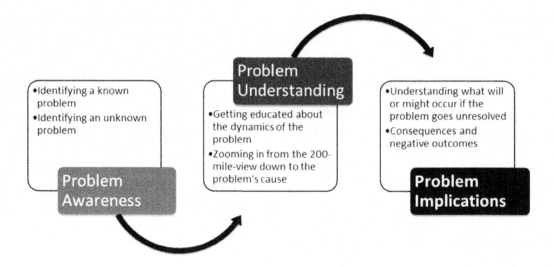

The *Why* Chain

A smart ministry recognizes the importance of understanding the implications of the problems it solves.

- Why?
  - o People are not compelled to solve problems until they understand the negative consequence(s) that will or might result if the problems go unresolved. This is true for both physical and spiritual problems.
- Why?
  - o Problem implications expose risks or dangers, as well as provide clarity on the best solution(s) to implement.

Rhyme *for* Reason

- ❖ *A problem's implications*
- ❖ *Show why the problem must be solved.*
- ❖ *Speeding up the need for solutions*
- ❖ *So that issues can be resolved.*

- ❖ *Knowing why solutions are needed*
- ❖ *Can help your ministry support,*
- ❖ *Those you serve or partner with*
- ❖ *In situations of any sort.*

Scriptural Application

<u>Bible Verse</u>

John 8:24 – "I told you that you would die in your sins; if you do not believe that I am he, you will indeed die in your sins."

<u>Commentary</u>

There is no greater "problem implication" than the result of not believing that Jesus is the Son of God. All physical problems have temporal implications, meaning that they cease to exist when we die. Spiritual problems, however, have eternal implications. As expressed in John 8:24, failure to have a personal relationship with Jesus causes one to die in their sins, ultimately resulting in eternal separation from God. While the Gospel is centered on the love, passion, and grace that God has for us, there are also extreme implications if people choose not to accept His free gift of salvation. By teaching about these implications, Jesus makes it clear what *will* happen to those that reject His eternal gift.

See pages 175-183 for "Action Questions" related to this principle.

CHAPTER 6

Solution Benefits

"There is always a solution to every problem. Find opportunities in circumstance. Never become a victim." – Lailah Gifty Akita

Solutions are meant to solve problems and create benefits. Michael Gerber, "The World's #1 Small Business Guru," states in his book, *E-Myth Mastery*, that customers purchase products or services (solutions) based on their "attractive" or "avoidance" benefits.[16] Attractive benefits are the positive outcomes that will result from the solution. Avoidance benefits are the negative consequences (problem implications) that the solution will help avoid.

I'd like to take this concept a step further and say that, in general, a solution's benefits, regardless of whether something is being sold or not, should have attractive and avoidance benefits. Here is an example in business:

Problem	Problem Implications	Solution	Benefits
A car manufacturer is receiving reports of faulty brake systems in thousands of vehicles.	Faulty brake systems risk damaging the manufacturer's reputation of making safe and reliable vehicles. Additionally, customer injury or death could result from such issues.	Implementing a mass recall to inspect each vehicle, fix issues with upgraded parts, and ensure customers that the safety risks have been addressed.	Re-instilling consumer confidence in the brand's safety and reliability (attractive benefit), avoiding customer injury or casualties (avoidance benefit), and creating brand loyalty by showing customers that problems are addressed quickly and in ways that exceed expectations (attractive benefit).

---

[16] Michael E. Gerber, *E-Myth Mastery* (New York City: Harper-Collins Publishers, 2006), 141.

Tom Vande Guchte, CEO of Storr Office Environments, describes this principle as it relates to his business.

> *For over 100 years, Storr's mission has been to be the single source solution for creating inspiring workspaces. We provide creative solutions for our customers related to design and space planning, flooring, furnishings, installation, and more by providing their employees a workspace where they can be engaged and inspired. Office environments should support the culture and brand of the company. At Storr, we strive to help our clients create workplaces that are a tangible representation of their corporate identity.*
>
> *When Storr turns our client's visions into reality, they benefit in numerous ways. Workplaces that have inspiring design elements help attract new employees, increase employee engagement, and therefore increase workplace productivity. Inspiring workplaces are not limited to only creative designs, but to practical designs as well. For some clients, the layout of their workplace has direct correlation to how efficiently they can accomplish their tasks. Storr's practical workplace solutions benefit our clients by helping them avoid inefficiencies that may have previously resulted in unnecessary risks or costs. Each Storr client is unique—therefore, no matter what solution we provide, our focus is delivering the client their unique desired results. Operating a business or ministry means you exist to provide beneficial solutions—doing so will enable any organization to achieve its goals.*

Like businesses, Christian ministries need to clearly communicate the benefits their solutions provide—benefits that generate positive outcomes and/or help people avoid negative consequences (problem implications).

Partners International's President and CEO, Larry Andrews, describes how this principle is a key driver in his ministry's operations:

> *One of the ways that Partners International measures the effectiveness of our solutions is by creating key metrics that gauge the results we are producing in areas such as quantity of churches planted, quantity of leaders trained, strength of relationships with indigenous ministry partners, financial partners, and more. Our objective is to create a holistic view of our desired outcomes through measurement systems we create and manage. This helps us in our decision making to ensure that we are always improving to help our ministry partners reduce risks and experience positive outcomes both on spiritual and physical levels.*
>
> *We are deeply engaged with our ministry partners around the world and speak/meet with them extensively. Our ministry is about connecting people and organizations in the western church with ministry organizations in the least reached places in the world—with a specific goal to strengthen, accelerate, and maximize the advancement of the Kingdom.*

This is a spiritual outcome that is primarily attributed to the benefits our ministry's solutions create, which are essential to building strong, trusting relationships.

Our ultimate goal is to ensure that we are fulfilling our vision and achieving our mission. Every solution we put in place is linked to our organizational goals and we measure their effectiveness to achieve desired outcomes through metrics, reporting, and operating with a continuous improvement mindset. Christian ministries should determine what outcomes they are striving to produce. This will help them create solutions that benefit both their ministry and the people they impact so that they stay on course to accomplish their goals.

Benefits of the Gospel

Sharing the Gospel and creating disciples of Jesus Christ should be a common mission that all Christian ministries share. The following is an example of how properly utilizing this principle can help communicate the benefits of accepting Jesus as Lord and Savior.

When you are presenting the Gospel, the following might be part of what you would communicate:
1. Making sure that God's true identity is properly understood so that any misperceptions about Him are resolved, using Scripture to support who God is and who God isn't.
2. Providing an overview of the Bible and addressing key points in chronological order to help set the context for the subsequent points.
3. Ensuring that your audience clearly understands the problem that every person is born with—sin (problem awareness).
4. Defining what sin is and ensuring your audience understands both the temporal and eternal implications of unforgiven sin—what *will* happen if they do not accept God's free gift of eternal salvation (problem implications).
5. Introducing the perfect and only solution to everyone's sin problem—Jesus Christ.

While it is not our words that save, but the power of the Holy Spirit alone, we should still communicate the benefits of placing one's faith in Jesus to non-believers. This will ensure that they understand what it means to follow Christ. The following outlines seven benefits of having a personal relationship with Jesus, which are all supported by Scripture:

1. Your relationship with God is restored, resulting in no condemnation (*positive outcome and avoided consequence*) (Romans 8:1).
2. The Holy Spirit dwells within you and begins to change you from the inside out. You have the power to transform your mind and your desires to align with God's desires (*positive outcome*) (1 Corinthians 6:19; Romans 12:2).

3. You are guaranteed a place in Heaven when you die. No matter how hard your circumstances may be, you can hold strong to this assured, eternal hope (*positive outcome*) (John 3:15; Titus 1:2).
4. You are no longer defenseless against the powers of sin and temptation from the devil. You are filled with the same Holy Spirit that enabled Jesus to defeat both sin and death (*positive outcome and avoided consequence*) (Ephesians 6:11).
5. Even during times of loneliness, you can be assured that God is with you, will never leave you, and will never forsake you (*positive outcome*) (Hebrews 13:5).
6. You are part of God's family and are called His child. You are loved and cherished as a son or daughter by the Creator of the Universe (*positive outcome*) (Galatians 3:26).
7. You are a key part of God's redemption plan to help lead the lost to a saving faith in Jesus Christ. There is no greater "cause" or "movement" to be a part of (*positive outcome*) (2 Corinthians 5:18-20).

In addition to communicating the benefits of the Gospel, understanding this principle will positively impact those within each of your ministry's Five Key Contexts.

Service Audience

Business Logic. While every product or service has different features, customers are ultimately buying the benefits that the features provide, not the features themselves. It is the feature's benefits (positive outcomes, avoided consequences, or both) that produce the customer's desired results.

> *For over 15 years, SPS delivered IT solutions to customers in retail, banking, food service, lodging, and government agencies in over 100 countries around the world. Our solutions included site surveys, risk analysis, cabling installations, electrical installations, wireless infrastructure set-up, and more. In SPS' business context, the two factors that motivated customers to make IT investments were: (1) the positive results the technology would create and (2) the risks that such technology would help reduce or eliminate for their organization.*

> *While SPS didn't sell wireless routers, we installed the cabling that made them operational, in addition to installing the routers as well. While we didn't sell ATMs, we set up the electrical, wireless infrastructure, and data cabling that enabled them to function properly. By providing solutions that delivered meaningful benefits, we were able to ensure that our customers achieved positive returns on their IT investments.*

Ministry Logic. Just as "if-then" statements are helpful to understanding a problem's implications, "so-that" statements can be helpful in understanding a solution's benefits.

Your ministry's solutions must provide meaningful benefits ***so that*** your service audience is motivated to solve their problems. "The confused mind says no" is a saying in business that has direct application to ministries as well. Sometimes solutions can be overthought, thus making them complicated and difficult to understand. Ultimately, solutions should be mirror images of problems. If the service audience's problem is a lack of awareness of who Jesus is, the solution should be creating opportunities to make them aware of Him. The benefits of knowing Jesus are numerous as listed in the previous section. If a service audience's problem is malnutrition or lack of clean water, the solution is to provide them with a sustainable food source and access to clean water. The benefits of these solutions are reduced health risks, increased work productivity, economic development, and more. For every problem your ministry addresses, don't assume your service audience understands how they will benefit from your solutions. Tell them, and do it repeatedly over time.

Jonathan Wiles, VP for Program Excellence with Living Water International, references examples of how Living Water uses this principle within its ministry context:

> *When dealing with a complex web of physical and spiritual problems, Living Water strives for consistent benefits in our programs, but in ways that are contextualized to what God is already doing in a particular place.*
>
> *Since we believe that the root cause of both physical and spiritual poverty is broken relationships, we do our work in a very relational way. In particular, we focus on the role of local churches. God plants local congregations within communities to serve as His hands, feet, and voice—demonstrating and proclaiming the Gospel and exercising what Paul calls the "ministry of reconciliation" (2 Cor. 5:18-21). One of the critical results we seek through the work that we do is for churches to thrive, being better equipped for life and work.*
>
> *The lasting benefit of water, sanitation, and hygiene being addressed in this kind of relational way is multi-faceted. Safe water reduces waterborne disease in communities by 17%, but improving hygiene practices (like hand washing) over time cuts these diseases by 48%.[17] Having water close to home keeps kids healthy and in school. Mothers are able to grow vegetables and turn their time savings into income.*
>
> *A community that is empowered in this way is able to manage its resources better, sustain gains that have been made, be more resilient when disasters strike, and ultimately be a signpost to God's Kingdom—pointing people to the restorative power of God's love. Every Christian ministry should focus on implementing practical solutions that help reduce risks and create positive outcomes for those it serves.*

---

[17] Cairncross, et al., 2010, "Water, sanitation and hygiene for the prevention of diarrhoea," *International Journal of Epidemiology*: http://ije.oxfordjournals.org/content/39/suppl_1/i193.full

Financial Partners

Business Logic. Investors are interested in businesses that clearly understand what factors motivate their customer's purchasing decisions. When this is understood, sales and marketing strategies are based on what the customer values, which makes them highly relevant, meaningful, and attractive. Businesses that understand what results their customers are seeking, and provide solutions that deliver the desired benefits, will effectively capture investor interest.

Ministry Logic. It is essential to educate your financial partners on the benefits their investments will create **so that** they are motivated to support your ministry. Financial investments produce positive outcomes including (1) equipping your ministry to capitalize on unique service opportunities, (2) creating new capabilities to broaden your outreach, and (3) enabling your ministry to hire the staff it needs. Financial investments will also help your ministry invest in resources to reduce risks that may affect those internal or external to your organization.

Volunteers

Business Logic. Businesses partner with suppliers because they have problems they are unable to solve themselves. By having awareness of their problems, as well as understanding the implications of each, businesses will have clarity on the solutions and benefits they need suppliers to provide. Many suppliers solve the same problems, but what separates one from another is the benefits their solutions create. If a supplier can solve a business's problems in better ways than its competitors, it will gain a competitive advantage that positions it for long-term success.

Ministry Logic. Volunteers must clearly understand how they will benefit your ministry **so that** they are motivated to sacrifice their time to serve others. For some volunteers, their sole source of motivation is knowing that their service pleases God. Others may need/want additional information in order to understand how their participation benefits others. Volunteers help ministries do more in less time, at low to no cost, which reduces the financial risks of operating a ministry solely based on utilizing staff. They also provide subject matter expertise that can benefit a particular service audience in numerous ways. As an example, if a ministry serves teen mothers who are considering aborting unplanned pregnancies, volunteers who have experience in this circumstance can provide empathetic, wise council. When recruiting volunteers, don't assume they know how they will benefit your ministry. Make them fully aware in order to maximize their motivation to serve.

Strategic Partners

Business Logic. The goal of a strategic partner relationship is to form an alliance where two businesses benefit by reducing risks and achieving positive outcomes together. At the beginning stages of the partnership, it is critical that both businesses understand how each will benefit so that the possibility of future success motivates them to work together. Strategic partnerships may solve financial problems that two businesses have. By joining together, they are able to increase sales and reduce fixed or variable costs, which increases the bottom line and makes each business more financially sound. Strategic partnerships may also solve operational problems. By partnering together, businesses can streamline operations through an efficient organizational structure. A benefit of streamlining operations is stronger customer service capabilities, which may be critical to ensuring the businesses remain competitive.

Ministry Logic. Strategic partnerships should benefit both ministries ***so that*** common goals can be pursued with commitment and passion. Two ministries may partner together in order to strengthen operational weaknesses. One ministry may have staffing needs that a strategic partnership can solve. The other ministry may need subject matter expertise that can be leveraged through the partnership. While the original intent of the strategic partnership might have been to solve each other's operational problems, the partnership can ultimately serve broader functions as well. By leveraging each other's strengths, each ministry will be better positioned to solve their service audience's problems through faster response times, additional subject matter expertise, and more.

Staff

Business Logic. For a business to be successful, it needs employees who are confident in solving problems. Business plans, sales objectives, and customer service protocols are great, however, the true value of a business's staff is revealed when things do not go according to plan. When plans are disrupted, the options are to panic and give up or to run towards problems with a solution mindset. Every problem has a solution and being in business is about solving problems, managing risks, and creating positive outcomes on a daily basis. Having efficient problem solvers on staff will enable any business to create competitive advantages that are difficult to replicate.

Ministry Logic. It is essential to build your ministry with solution-oriented staff ***so that*** it continuously moves forward in a positive direction. Being solution-oriented means that your staff members stay calm and avoid "analysis paralysis" when things go wrong. It also means they remain hopeful that every problem has a solution, which is critical in order to instill hope in others. Daniel Goleman, author of the book, *Emotional Intelligence*, says that "from the perspective of emotional intelligence, having hope means that one will not give in to overwhelming anxiety, a defeatist attitude, or depression in the face of difficult challenges or setbacks."[18] Regardless of the situation, having a positive mindset when facing problems will enable clarity of thought, proper perspective when praying, and a belief that every problem can be solved.

No matter how well you understand the principles within this book and no matter how strong you are in your faith, problems will always be present on this side of eternity. Don't be fearful when problems arise—learn to manage your fear so that problems are addressed in accordance to their severity. Develop

---

[18] Daniel Goleman, *Emotional Intelligence* (New York City: Bantam Books, 1995), 87.

a joy for understanding and solving problems and focus on creating solutions that avoid negative consequences and/or result in positive outcomes.

Visualize

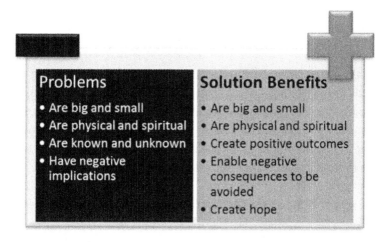

The *Why* Chain

A smart ministry understands the importance of creating beneficial solutions across its Five Key Contexts.

- Why?
  - o If problems are not solved with the appropriate solutions, they can grow into larger issues.
- Why?
  - o Unless the causes of the problems are known, and their implications understood, it is difficult to implement solutions that deliver meaningful benefits.

Rhyme *for* Reason

- ❖ *Problems act as guidelines,*
- ❖ *Helping determine what to do.*
- ❖ *Their implications create clarity,*
- ❖ *On which solution to pursue.*

- ❖ *A solution's benefits are positive,*
- ❖ *Producing outcomes people need,*
- ❖ *And remove risk or danger,*
- ❖ *Giving hope to you and me.*

Scriptural Application

<u>Bible Verse</u>

John 10:28 – "I give them eternal life, and they shall never perish; no one will snatch them out of my hand."

<u>Commentary</u>

Throughout the Gospels, Jesus often communicates the benefits of following Him. John 10:28 is one example, and His words are extremely encouraging. From this verse alone, Jesus outlines three benefits for those that believe in Him. First, we will have eternal life (positive outcome). Second, we will never perish (avoided consequence). Third, no one will ever snatch us out of Jesus' hand (positive outcome and avoided consequence). While our minds can't fathom the true magnificence of these benefits, everyone who places their faith in Jesus is assured of this eternal, unwavering hope.

See pages 175-183 for "Action Questions" related to this principle.

Summary: Chapters 1-6

The 12 Principles of *The Smart Ministry* are essentially "solution benefit principles." The following are examples of solution benefit statements that summarize the first six principles covered thus far:

1. Ministry leaders create a vision, mission, and strategy for their organization *so that* they are clear on why they exist, what they want to achieve, and how they will achieve it.
2. Market intelligence is gathered *so that* a ministry can define its target service audiences, understand how to best serve them, and stay focused in order to maximize its outreach efficiency and effectiveness.
3. Smart ministries understand what credibility factors are most important *so that* they are able to develop trusting relationships within each of their Five Key Contexts.
4. Ministries need to understand problems at macro and micro levels *so that* they are clear on the proper solutions to implement.
5. Ministries need to understand the implications of the problems they face *so that* they can proactively prevent negative outcomes.
6. Successful ministries ensure that their solutions deliver meaningful benefits *so that* risks are avoided and positive outcomes are achieved.

CHAPTER 7

Strategic Positioning

"Do not free a camel of the burden of his hump; you may be freeing him from being a camel." — G.K. Chesterton

In the book, *Business Model Generation*, it states that a business model "describes the rationale of how an organization creates, delivers, and captures value."[19] There are numerous elements in the business model equation, but perhaps the most important is the business's value proposition. A value proposition is the key driver in how a business strategically positions itself in the marketplace, which shapes its corporate identity, brand, and market reputation. A value proposition is essentially how the business creates value for its customers by solving their problems and delivering benefits that are superior to the competition. At the heart of a business's value proposition is *uniqueness*. This distinguishing factor enables a business to deliver value that is difficult for others to emulate. The business with a superior value proposition has an advantage within the markets it competes in, and it leverages its uniqueness to drive sales, growth, and profitability.

Bandwidth Co-founder and Executive Chairman, Henry Kaestner, has leveraged the value of this principle in his company as expressed in the following statement:

> There are many telecom solutions providers in our industry, however, Bandwidth has created our reputation not only based on what we do, but on how we do it. Our business division provides solutions for our customers that include setting up Toll Free Numbers, call tracking/monitoring, and unique smart phone applications. Our consumer division is backed by Republic Wireless® and RingTo, which provide unlimited data, talk and text service, in addition to a unique method of moving our clients' mobile phone numbers to the cloud.
>
> At Bandwidth, we believe in creating an environment for our employees that is motivating, inspiring, and where no idea is too big or small to be considered. The unique value we

---

[19] Alexander Osterwalder and Yves Pigneur, *Business Model Generation* (Hoboken: John Wiley & Sons, Inc., 2010), 14.

provide our customers, investors, and business partners starts with the corporate culture we have created—one that promotes idea creation and judgment free environments that give our people the opportunities to help propel Bandwidth into the future. I would advise any business or ministry to embrace what makes them unique and to exercise their God-given right to serve in ways that creates unique value for others.

Most Christian ministries don't view competition, value propositions, and differentiation in the same ways that businesses do. Nor should they. All businesses have at least one common goal—to generate profitable revenue. It is within this goal where business-to-business competition resides. Just as businesses share a common goal of profitable revenue, all Christian ministries should share the common goal of fulfilling the Great Commission and creating disciples of Jesus Christ. So if a Christian ministry has distinctive qualities that enable it to deliver unique value, can it promote its uniqueness without appearing to be in competition with other ministries? Absolutely! God is the Creator of creativity, and I believe every ministry should identify, create, and develop its uniqueness in order to bless others and honor God.

Just as a business's "business model" represents how it delivers value to its customers, a ministry's "ministry model" represents how it delivers unique value to its service audiences and other key contexts. A ministry model includes defining who the service audiences are, how they can best be served, the outreach channels through which the ministry serves, the financial needs of the ministry, key personnel needed, and more. All of the components of a ministry model should work together to create value for others and point them to Jesus.

The JESUS Film Project understands the importance of strategic positioning. Josh Newell, Director of Marketing and Communications, provided the following statement outlining how his ministry uses its unique ministry model to advance the Gospel:

One of the benefits of our ministry model is that we use technology to help scale our operations, enabling us to reach more people in geographically dispersed locations in less time. Over the course of our existence, our use of technology has enabled us to share the Gospel with over six billion people, translate our films and audio resources into over 1,300 languages, distribute over 60 million evangelistic resources, and receive over 200 million indications of people giving their lives to Jesus. We are uniquely blessed to have been used by God in so many ways, and we pray daily that He enables us to continue our service in helping to fulfill the Great Commission.

With the rapid advancement of technology in recent times, we have capitalized on some of these technological breakthroughs to help us strengthen how we position our ministry globally. Mobile technology has given us the opportunity to reinvent the distribution channels we use to share our resources and spread the Gospel. We have created a mobile platform that not only hosts our videos, but allows others to access them at no cost. This has resulted in a more efficient way to spread the Gospel through working with thousands of strategic partners (ministries and lay people) that evangelize through digital media and follow through with personal discipleship and on-the-ground ministry. Once we moved beyond our website being the central access point of our resources, the viewership of our films has skyrocketed through various partnerships with organizations such as YouVersion and others.

The JESUS Film Project celebrates the unique platform we have been given to serve God and others. Every Christian ministry should identify their unique areas of influence and use it to serve God and impact people's lives.

Service Audience

Business Logic. Similar to any business strategy, value propositions can be categorized at a high-level, however, their specific application can be infused into any business context. Examples of generic value propositions that spread across every commercial market include those that:

1. Lower a customer's variable costs (costs of goods sold) and/or lower their fixed costs (operating costs).
2. Increase the quality of a product or service that the customer needs or wants. Depending on the market and type of offer, some customers will pay more for superior quality. In other cases, some businesses will provide higher quality at lower prices. This one-two combination creates a very compelling value proposition.
3. Save customers time. "Time is money" is a common phrase in business, and it means that if you're not making money, you're losing money. Customers are always looking for ways to increase the speed of what they do, which leads to saving time and money.
4. Reduce customer risks. Every customer has some awareness of the risks it faces across various contexts. When a business can reduce a customer's known risks or proactively reduce unknown risks, it has a strong value proposition.
5. Provide unparalleled customer service. Businesses that sell commodity goods can separate themselves from the competition by providing superior customer service. When a business can quickly resolve customer issues, while making them feel valued and appreciated, loyal and long-term customer relationships are created.

Some business leaders would argue that you need to pick one type of value proposition and focus most of your efforts in that area (while still being competitive in other key areas). I agree, depending on the context. In some markets, being the very best at one thing is enough to set a business apart from the competition. In other markets, a business may need to be the best in two or more areas to deliver superior value to its customers. Creating this type of value proposition isn't easy and it can require significant investments. No matter what market conditions a business may face, its value proposition should be based on what is *most meaningful to the market*. This is a stumbling block for many businesses because they offer solutions they perceive as valuable without verifying what the market deems as valuable.

When I started at SPS, the company had a reputation of being one of, if not the best, at what it did. For years, SPS' reputation was based on being able to consistently deliver the highest quality IT solutions, no matter where the customer site was located. In any given year, SPS deployed IT solutions at over 15,000 customer sites spanning across 100+ countries.

There's an idiom in business that says, "speed, quality, and cost—pick two." In 2007, market conditions were becoming extremely competitive and being the best at one (or even two) wasn't enough to retain and acquire new customers. In response to the evolving markets, our company leaders invested in new assets that strengthened our value proposition and enabled us to offer the highest quality IT solutions faster than anyone else, and at the lowest prices. Our new and unique value proposition attracted customers, deterred competitors, intrigued suppliers, and helped us recruit top talent.

For a business to ensure the right value proposition is in place, it must start by understanding the market(s) it competes in. Value propositions are generally created based upon the market intelligence that a business gathers. If a business understands the market's needs and perceptions, as well as how to deliver unique solutions and benefits, it will create a value proposition that helps it stand out from the crowd.

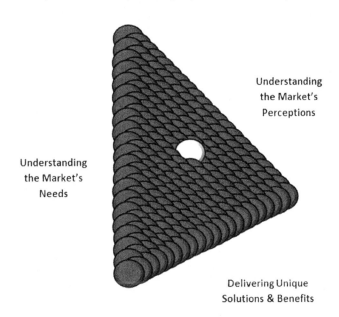

Understanding the Market's Perceptions

Understanding the Market's Needs

Delivering Unique Solutions & Benefits

Ministry Logic. If your ministry serves multiple service audiences, you may have discovered that each service audience needs to be served in a specific way to maximize the value that is created for them. This may require a specific ministry model for each service audience, and if so, this will require a specific value proposition as well. Ministries should use the intelligence they've gathered relative to each service audience in order to understand how to most effectively serve them. The key, however, is to ensure that your ministry model and value proposition do not compromise God's Word for the sake of contemporary relevance.

Global Media Outreach utilizes the platform of technology to take the Gospel to the nations. Kathy Gray, Marketing Manager for GMO, provided the following comments in regard to how GMO uses their ministry model to impact people's lives for the Gospel:

> *Walt Wilson, GMO Founder and Chairman, said, "We are the first generation in history to hold in our hands the technology to fulfill the Great Commission." As Christians, we have the honor of being called to preach God's message to every nation. At GMO, our unique attributes strategically position us to fulfill our mission to reach the world for Christ. We understand why we exist, where we are headed, and how we will get there as described by our three Core Values:*
>
> - ***SHARE*** *– Giving everyone on Earth multiple opportunities to know Jesus.*
> - ***GROW*** *– Building them in their faith.*
> - ***CONNECT****- Connecting them to a Christian community.*
>
> *GMO is unique in our ability to effectively navigate a changing world by using technology to reach people in every nation with the Good News of Jesus. In order to effectively reach the lost in every nation, our ministry model is built upon standard operating procedures that have the flexibility to be customized based on who we are ministering to. Our use of technology enables us to offer anonymous intimacy to those looking for answers to life's greatest questions, many of which come from countries where people can be killed for being a Christian. As a key element of our ministry model, more than 6,000 volunteer Online Missionaries provide discipleship in 26 languages. We understand that taking the Gospel to the world requires approaches that cater to people from different countries, languages, faiths, and more. Our Online Missionaries help us meet people where they are, guide them into a growing relationship with Christ, and connect them to a local Christian community. After sharing Jesus with more than a billion people in the last decade and having more than 100 million people indicate a decision for Christ, we know lives are being transformed and we measure the transformations through a tool we've created called the "Christian Growth Index."*
>
> *The pace that our world is changing is creating new opportunities for evangelism and discipleship that have never been present before. While GMO continues to make Jesus known to a changing world, every Christian ministry should identify and live out their unique calling to serve, evangelize, and disciple others in order to fulfill the Great Commission.*
>
> > *"And this Gospel of the Kingdom will be preached in the whole world as a testimony to all nations, and then the end will come." – Matthew 24:14*

Financial Partners

Business Logic. Investors have many different motivations and criteria for investing. However, there is a common investment evaluation tool called the "MAR Model", which stands for "**M**arket, **A**dvantages, **R**eturns." Investors want to be sure that the business they are investing in has a thorough understanding of the markets ("M") it competes in. Investors also want to be clear on the advantages ("A") the business has over its competition and how those advantages will translate into superior customer value. Lastly, investors want to understand their potential return ("R"), based on the business's valuation (which translates into the investor's equity ownership) as well as sales and profitability projections. No matter what an investor's investment criteria is, a business with a strong value proposition and unique strategic positioning strategy will succeed at securing the required investments.

Ministry Logic. Having a structured ministry model, defined value proposition, and effective strategic positioning strategy will help any ministry obtain the funds it needs. Like business investors, most financial partners like to be diversified in their giving. Since there are so many ministries doing similar work, it is common for financial partners to ask, "What makes your ministry different?" when evaluating where to give their funds. This question can be answered in various ways—however, the financial partner is really looking to understand what the ministry does to serve others in unique and highly effective ways. It's a legitimate question, and whether or not it's asked, it is most likely being thought about. Financial partners ultimately want to invest in ministries that are biblically sound, that love Jesus, and that create new levels of value for those they are serving.

As mentioned in an earlier section, I'm not suggesting that ministries promote themselves over others in the form of competition. However, every ministry should be promoting the attributes that make it uniquely qualified to serve in effective and efficient ways. As an adaptation to the "MAR Model", ministries can utilize the AUR Method—**A**udience, **U**niqueness, **R**esults. When used in the context of financial partners, a ministry should present the knowledge it has about its target service *audience* (A) to show financial partners that it understands whom it is serving. A ministry can then demonstrate how it is able to serve them in *unique* (U) ways and outline the *results* (R) that are expected from its outreach. This simple method of presenting how a ministry's outreach model functions will provide financial partners assurance that their investments will bear fruit that has temporal and eternal value.

Volunteers

Business Logic. In many cases, a business's value proposition has extensive reliance upon its supply chain. Most businesses depend on multiple suppliers to deliver high value solutions to their customers. Even suppliers of commodity products are critical to a business's value proposition because these simple products can be vital to the business's unique offering.

Ministry Logic. Volunteers are essential to nearly every ministry's value proposition. The uniqueness of your ministry may be attributed to the strength of your volunteer chain. Like business suppliers, volunteers are a critical component to your ministry's ability to create and deliver distinctive value for others. Volunteers provide unique insight, offer low/no cost solutions to staffing problems, and enable ministries to do more with less people. Assess your ministry model to identify how you are currently leveraging your volunteers as well as how you can further utilize them to create added value.

Strategic Partners

Business Logic. Two organizations with unique value propositions can create an even stronger competitive advantage by joining together as a single entity for a common purpose. Sometimes, the only way for a business to increase its market share is by joining forces with another business. That other business may be a customer, supplier, or even a competitor. Gaining market share and competitive dominance takes time if done organically within a single business. However, partnering with other organizations that have similar objectives joins two unique value propositions and raises the probability of success.

Ministry Logic. If your ministry has an opportunity to partner with one or more organizations, a key factor to the success of the strategic partnership is understanding the unique qualities that each ministry offers. The beauty of strategic partnerships is that, by joining together, each party can instantly leverage the other's uniqueness to deliver additional value to service audiences, financial partners, staff members, and/or volunteers. Think about your ministry's goals and whether the creation of strategic partnerships can help expedite the achievement of those goals.

Partners International strategically positions itself as a ministry that is taking the Gospel to the least reached regions of the world through the platform of strategic partnerships. The following is a statement provided by Larry Andrews, President and CEO of Partners International, which summarizes how they leverage the value of this principle within their ministry:

> *Differentiation is critical to create identity, value, and clarity on the key focus areas of an organization. Partners International's strategic positioning defines why we are able to do what we are called to in a way that differentiates us from other ministries. People want to invest in organizations that clearly understand what differentiates them from others and how that differentiation creates unique value for the people they serve and partner with. Clarity on a ministry's strategic position helps align the right partners that believe in the vision, mission, and strategy, while excluding people who do not. Here are some of the key unique factors of the Partners International ministry that help us establish and develop relationships with like-minded people and organizations:*
>
> - ***Years of Experience, Effectiveness, and Impact.*** *We have been a pioneer and recognized leader in mission partnerships with indigenous ministries since 1943— that's over 70 years of trust and impact.*

- **Partnership Synergy Impact Model**. *We identify high-impact, indigenous Christian ministries and partner with them in accountable, trusting partnerships to advance God's Kingdom in the least reached regions of the world.*
- **Sustained Capacity Building**. *We go far beyond providing just financial resources. We focus on capacity building through focused training and equipping, leadership development, strategic planning, and ongoing counsel that helps our partners become successful, sustainable organizations that are transforming their communities and nations for Christ.*
- **Holistic "Gospel-Centered" Ministry Approach**. *Our key strategy to reach and impact lives is holistic witness, which means reaching out to the "whole" person. We address physical, spiritual, and socio-economic concerns with the Gospel message of hope. This is how we pick our partners.*
- **Global Scale**. *We work in 58 nations in partnership with more than 110 indigenous Christian ministries.*

If Christian ministries can create something that is unique, they can succeed in creating both perceived and real value for everyone they interact with, which is critical in a world with so many choices of where to invest finances, time, talent, and resources.

Staff

Business Logic. A business's value proposition and strategic position create a perception that either attracts or discourages top talent from wanting to be part of its team. I recently read about a relatively small event planning company who had over 10,000 applicants apply for a single job position. Their company's value proposition has created a unique corporate culture, and therefore a strategic position within their market, that attracts talented candidates who want to be part of what their organization is doing.

Ministry Logic. Most ministries need unique competencies kept in-house in order to maintain desired levels of quality control. A ministry's "ministry model" and unique value proposition can be the driving factors behind attracting the most qualified staff. The right staff members work together to create, refine, and deliver value that benefits others and honors God with what He has called them to do.

Your ministry may already have various factors that make it unique. If you haven't identified its uniqueness yet, no need to worry. By working hard, working smart, and asking God for wisdom, favor, and direction, you'll be surprised at how quickly you can create an identity for your ministry that helps it stand out while remaining aligned with God's Word.

Visualize

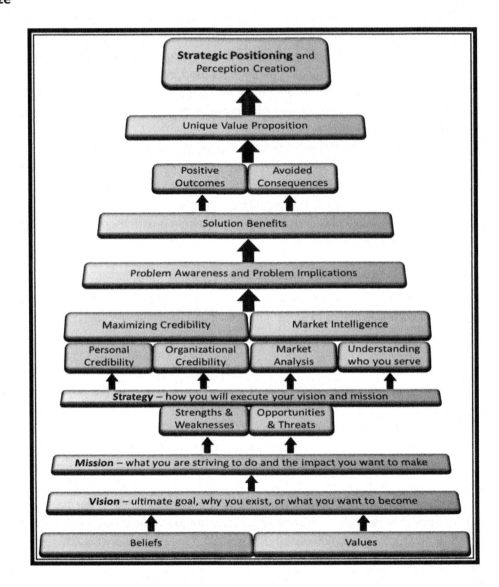

The *Why* Chain

A smart ministry understands the importance of strategic positioning.

- Why?
    - o A ministry's strategic position is created by how it wants to be perceived and by understanding the value it wants to deliver. Understanding both are essential for a ministry's short and long-term viability.

- Why?
    - o People want to be associated with ministries that offer unique value to others, as long as that uniqueness does not compromise God's Word.
- Why?
    - o Delivering unique value creates new opportunities to honor God and serve others.

Rhyme *for* Reason

❖ *Your ministry model*
❖ *And its value proposition,*
❖ *Should reflect your ministry's unique*
❖ *Vision and/or mission.*

❖ *Promote how your ministry is different*
❖ *Without compromising God's Word,*
❖ *Because relevance with compromise*
❖ *Creates perceptions that are blurred.*

Scriptural Application

Bible Verses

Matthew 16:15-17 – "'But what about you?' he asked. 'Who do you say I am?' Simon Peter answered, '"You are the Messiah, the Son of the living God.' Jesus replied, 'Blessed are you, Simon son of Jonah, for this was not revealed to you by flesh and blood, but by my Father in heaven.'"

Commentary – Strategic Positioning

Throughout the Gospels, it is interesting to see how Jesus referred to Himself when speaking to others. In other words, how He positioned Himself in the hearts and minds of those He interacted with. In some situations, Jesus performed a miracle, but instructed the receiver not to tell others what He had done. In other situations, Jesus boldly declared who He was by calling Himself the Son of God and other names that only He could claim. As the Creator of man and the human mind, Jesus understood (and understands) that people believe what they choose to believe. It is only through God's Spirit that we can begin to understand the true identity of who Jesus is. This is what happened to Peter in Matthew 16:15-17. Peter had seen and heard the same things that many others experienced. However, not all believed. Jesus revealed (and reveals) the truth about Himself through words, actions, and the Holy Spirit, while giving people the freedom to choose how they respond.

<u>Bible Verses</u>

Luke 24:33-35 – "They got up and returned at once to Jerusalem. There they found the Eleven and those with them, assembled together and saying, 'It is true! The Lord has risen and has appeared to Simon.' Then the two told what had happened on the way, and how Jesus was recognized by them when he broke the bread."

<u>Commentary – The Uniqueness of Jesus</u>

As Christians, we understand that our faith is not based on "religion" as the world defines it, but rather based on a personal relationship with Jesus Christ. This alone sets Christianity apart from any other organized religion or faith in existence. Another distinguishing attribute of our faith is that Jesus was resurrected from the dead. Luke 24: 33-35, along with other passages of the Gospels and the New Testament, regard the Resurrection as the cornerstone of the Christian faith. If Jesus was not already credible enough with the wisdom He displayed and the miracles He performed, the true test of His credibility was the Resurrection. He didn't disappoint. The Resurrection of Jesus is a fundamental and unique factor of the Christian faith, and it is the foundation upon which we stand.

*See pages 184-187 for "Action Questions" related to this principle.

CHAPTER 8

Interest Generation

"Curiosity is the wick in the candle of learning." — *William Arthur Ward*

I've always thought that the nightly news should be called "Bad News at 11." News stations seem to focus their reporting efforts on stories that revolve around accidents, tragedies, scandals, deaths, and disasters. Why are they so obsessed with the doom and gloom? There are two reasons. First, we live in a fallen world, so there is naturally an abundance of misfortune to report on. Second, news stations are after ratings, and it's these kinds of stories that drive ratings.

Have you ever considered the effectiveness of online search engines at generating interest? Their home pages are riddled with short titles that provide just enough information to pique one's interest. If the online visitor is curious enough, they'll click on the links to discover more. Being curious is an innate part of the human makeup, and this leads us to learn more about things that bother us or about things we don't understand.

Every successful business is effective at generating interest in the people it wants to influence. The purpose of this principle in business is to create sales opportunities and initiate relationships. If a customer is not interested in what a business offers, the business misses an opportunity to prove that its product or service can provide unique value. If investors are not interested in a business's value proposition, the business misses an opportunity to present why their company is an attractive investment. The ability to generate interest in others is a critical principle to understand if businesses want to create opportunities and relationships that will position their organizations for success.

Jim Anthony, Founder and CEO of Anthony & Company, shares his thoughts below on the value of this principle in his business:

> *Anthony & Co. has developed a reputation for executing successful real estate projects. As our company has grown, our market reputation has been a key contributor toward helping us create new business opportunities. That is the power of "brand equity"—being able to create trust with others even before formally engaging in a working relationship with them. While the equity of our brand is a business opportunity creator, it is critical*

to keep our business partners interested in working with us through every phase of our relationship with them.

Our business is built upon the foundations of faith, professionalism, trust, and mutual respect, and these values permeate each of the key contexts we operate in. Our business model enables us to clearly understand our customer's goals so that we can turn their problems into success stories. We leverage these success stories to generate interest in new clients, investors, staff, suppliers, and strategic partners. Additionally, our business is unique in that we are conscious of the "spiritual environment" of our workplace, and we are intentional about praying with one another and inviting Jesus into every aspect of our organization. Our workplace culture has helped attract talented workers who want to be part of a company that has a higher purpose than just creating profits. The ability to generate interest is a necessary principle for any business or ministry that wants to maximize its opportunities to positively impact people's lives.

If people aren't interested in why your ministry exists, what it does, and how it does it, there will be limited opportunity for growth or development apart from divine intervention. Johnny Evans, Eastern NC Director of FCA (Fellowship of Christian Athletes) discusses the importance of this principle in his ministry to create service and partnership opportunities:

Two core values of the FCA ministry are service and teamwork. We must earn the right to work as a team by serving others unconditionally. This was the approach the Lord Jesus took in His earthly ministry.

The infrastructure of the FCA ministry is geared for partnerships. We are a volunteer intensive ministry with very few full-time staff members. One way we attempt to generate interest from volunteers is through our community events—banquets, luncheons, and golf tournaments. These are good ways to inform and recruit potential volunteers to partner in our ministry. Another way to generate interest in potential partners is through social media and digital communications. We also encourage and depend upon grassroots interest generation amongst the student athletes through old fashioned "word of mouth"—one athlete telling another about the benefits of engaging in their local FCA huddle.

In order for the generation of interest to be done with integrity and absent of manipulation, it's imperative that Christian ministries be motivated for the sake of God's Kingdom and not their own.

As with most strategies, interest generation techniques are general in nature but can be applied to nearly any organizational context. Below are seven generic strategies commonly used in business that can be customized by any ministry to help generate interest in those within its Five Key Contexts: [20]

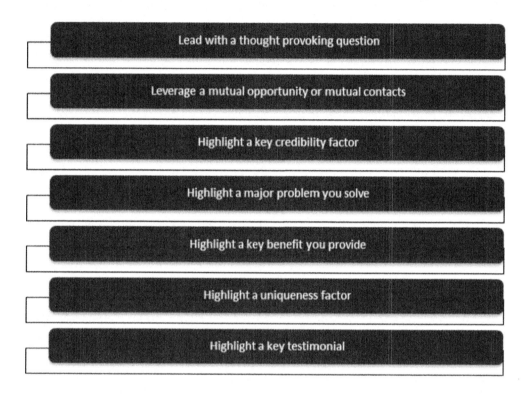

- Lead with a thought provoking question
- Leverage a mutual opportunity or mutual contacts
- Highlight a key credibility factor
- Highlight a major problem you solve
- Highlight a key benefit you provide
- Highlight a uniqueness factor
- Highlight a key testimonial

Service Audience

Business Logic. The sales strategy of every successful business is contingent upon its ability to generate interest in prospective customers. However, the real magic occurs when a business can take a generic strategy, customize it, and apply it to a specific context with meaningful relevance. For interest generation strategies to spark curiosity in prospective customers, businesses must understand what motivates their customers, what benefits they are seeking, what the competition is offering, etc. Today, people are busier than ever and are naturally impatient with businesses that are trying to "sell them something." An effective interest generation strategy is simple, meaningful, and piques the curiosity of customers enough so that they want to invest their time to learn more. In most cases, selling is a process, and generating interest in the minds of prospective customers initiates the process.

> *From 2008-2012, I spearheaded the development of a new business unit at SPS. When I*
> *started, I had limited business development experience and no sales partner to brainstorm*

---

[20] Thomas A. Freese, *Question Based Selling* (Naperville: Sourcebooks, Inc., 2000), 106-112.

with. I quickly learned that traditional "cold calling" would not produce the types of results I needed (and wanted).

After about two months with no results, I developed an interest generation strategy that created more sales opportunities than I could handle. I was targeting IT integrators—large, global organizations that typically outsourced to organizations like SPS for various IT solutions. After creating a list of 40 prospects, rather than cold calling them like a tele-marketer, I researched publically announced IT projects that we could potentially partner together on. By having this information, I was able to generate interest in the minds of my prospects, making them eager to listen and learn more about the opportunity.

Traditional cold calling statistics say that if you call 100 prospects, less than 10% will call you back. With the interest generation strategy I implemented, over 80% of the 40 prospects called me back within days of my initial communication. Of the 80% that called back, 90% resulted in face-to-face meetings to discuss the partnering opportunity. Within about eight months, I had established nine strategic partnerships with multi-million/billion dollar organizations, and it all started with an effective interest generation strategy.

Dave Jones, Co-founder of The Reset Agency describes the importance of this principle in his business:

The Reset Agency is unique in regards to the focus we have on helping organizations develop strategic vision and creating a culture that is passionate about achieving it. At our foundation, we exist to solve a problem that is widespread in the majority of organizations in the U.S—lack of direction. In response to this problem, we have created a methodology called the Reset Process (R7)™, which is designed to help organizations build a culture driven by passion and focused on vision. The name of our process itself generates curiosity in the minds of those we desire to serve, causing them to engage with us to learn more about how we might benefit them. The results of the Reset Process (R7)™ help our clients maximize their organizational efficiency and effectiveness through a solution-focused coaching model.

With our awareness of the lack of direction that exists in many organizations today, The Reset Agency feels compelled to want to generate interest in prospective customers to create opportunities to serve them. As every client has unique problems and circumstances, we take a collaborative approach by co-creating solutions. This method of collaboration has proved to be of high interest to our clients, as some of our competitors try to fit each client into a pre-defined process, which doesn't deliver the results the client needs.

Every business and ministry should exist to solve at least one problem—otherwise there is no need for the organization. They should believe in the solutions they provide and be motivated to generate interest in others to create service and partnership opportunities.

Ministry Logic. The key to generating interest in your service audience is to understand how they think and to learn what motivates them. Start by determining what your goal is for communicating with them. Do you want them to attend an event? Go to your website? Connect on social media? Respond to an email or call? There are many reasons why you will want to captivate their interest, and there are endless ways to customize the generic strategies listed above so that they are relevant to your contexts. When generating interest, it is essential to create messages that are relevant to whom you are targeting. In addition, it is important that the messages contain limited content, while simultaneously showing enough value to make the audience curious enough to want to learn more. As with all of the principles in this book, I believe there are always opportunities to be relevant without compromising God's Word. Use the market intelligence your ministry has gathered and create interest generation strategies based on that information. Select a group of people from your target service audience and ask them to validate the effectiveness of your strategies. If their feedback is positive, proceed. If it isn't, go back to the drawing board and co-create interest generation strategies with members of your service audience—this will minimize any assumptions about what interests them. Spending extra time to make sure your efforts are as relevant and strategic as possible will maximize the quantity of outreach opportunities you can create. It's the perfect balance of working hard and working smart.

Think about how you can customize the generic interest generation strategies to create outreach opportunities within your service audience context.

Financial Partners

Business Logic. Businesses utilize this principle throughout various stages of their relationships with investors. If a business is seeking an investment for operations or to pursue a new opportunity, it must understand how to capture the interest of prospective investors in order to initiate the process of gaining the investment. Strategies to pique investor interest usually begin with conversations about the specific opportunity, an executive summary of the business plan, and other high-level information. From there, it is common for the business to present its plans in more detail—details that the investor might not have fully understood if the information was presented too early in discussions. If investors are still interested, the business will then provide them with information outlining what they will get in return for their investment—equity ownership, business influence, etc. If the investor chooses to invest in the business, interest generation doesn't stop there. The business must keep their investors interested by updating them of progress and achievements. If the business needs additional funds in the future, existing investors are the best place to start.

Ministry Logic. Like a ministry's service audience, the types of financial partners it has will vary. Sometimes financial partners will be part of a ministry's service audience, and other times, the service audience and financial partners will be completely separate. In chapter two, we discussed why having market intelligence related to your service audience(s) enables the most efficient and effective outreach to be done. If your ministry can gain similar intelligence related to your financial partners, you will be better positioned to create meaningful and relevant interest generation strategies. If your ministry is unclear on what motivates them to invest, listed below are generic questions that every financial partner is interested in knowing the answers to:

1. What will my money be used for?
2. What are the desired end results and why is this important?
3. When will my money be used?
4. Who will be impacted?
5. How will they be impacted?
6. Will I receive updates on what my donations are helping to achieve?

> **Tip**: Provide your financial partners with "executive summary" updates outlining metrics, statistics, and other forms of high-level data they care most about seeing. Businessmen and women will especially appreciate this. Then, give them the opportunity to review additional detail if they want to learn more.

Build interest generation campaigns based on the answers to these questions, and think about how you can customize the generic interest generation strategies to initiate and retain donor relationships.

Volunteers

Business Logic. It is usually the supplier that captures a business's interest in order to create a working relationship. In some cases, however, businesses need to generate interest in suppliers. Suppliers that provide unique value are in high demand because they give businesses a competitive advantage. In such cases, businesses need to approach suppliers as they would a prospective customer—with strategies and tactics that make the suppliers interested in wanting to learn more about them. If a working relationship is established, the supplier's interest will remain as long as they benefit financially and/or strategically.

Motivation + **Interest** = Action.

Ministry Logic. A motivated group of volunteers can create immense value for your ministry by helping it accomplish more without incurring significant costs. To ensure that the right types and quantity of volunteers are attracted to service opportunities, ministries must understand how to generate interest in prospective volunteers, as well as how to keep current volunteers interested. Similar to the service audience and financial partner contexts, it will benefit your ministry to understand what motivates volunteers to sacrifice their time to serve. The quickest way to accomplish this is by speaking with your volunteers directly. Discover what motivates them to volunteer, which interest generation strategies are most relevant to your volunteer program, and work together to determine how to best attract and retain volunteers. Think about how you can customize the generic interest generation strategies to create opportunities within your ministry's volunteer context.

Lee Powell, Lead Pastor at Cedar Creek Church in Toledo, Ohio, provided the following comments about the value of this principle in regard to outreach and volunteer programs at his church:

> *One of the true joys in this life is loving and serving others. Leading people into a place where they can experience that joy is extremely rewarding! One such project we are involved in at Cedar Creek is "Impact NWO," a program that has enabled us to partner with several organizations, secular and non-secular, to eradicate hunger here in Northwest Ohio. Impact NWO is a food drive where food is collected and distributed to area food banks, soup kitchens, and other local organizations. We partner with numerous volunteers to organize, pack, and distribute the food. Their acts of humility, love, and service continually inspires Cedar Creek to create more opportunities as a church to love and serve our communities in Jesus' name. We have found the principle of "interest generation" to be a key ingredient in helping us mobilize the volunteers, church members, and strategic partners necessary to effectively serve the hungry in Northwest Ohio.*
>
> *Another example of how Cedar Creek leverages the value of this principle is by using it to create service opportunities for volunteers through a program we call "Test Drive." Through this program, we try to provide a variety of service opportunities so that volunteers with different gifts and desires can participate. In turn, this program helps us generate volunteer interest to serve. Every spring and fall, we ask prospective volunteers to fill out a Test Drive form which allows them to sign up for volunteer opportunities they are interested in. If they take a test drive and are interested in serving in other capacities, they are free to try another volunteer opportunity. The Test Drive process allows new volunteers to serve and connect with others as representatives of the Body of Christ.*
>
> *Generating interest in others creates service opportunities, helps initiate relationships, and unites people to pursue common goals. Properly understanding and applying this principle is critical to implementing God's calling for every Christian ministry.*

Strategic Partners

Business Logic. Initiating a strategic partnership is a lot like initiating a new customer account. It is not enough if only one business has interest in working with the other—there must be mutual interest. When developing a new customer account, the process begins with the sales person having interest in working with the prospective customer. Mutual interest is then gained when the prospect sees value in learning more about what the sales person is offering. Strategic partnerships are similar in that interest may start with only one party. However, it must develop into shared, mutual interest before a partnership can be established. From there, it is the manner in which the two businesses work together (and how they create value), that determines their interest in continuing to collaborate as partners.

Ministry Logic. Christian ministries may seek a strategic partnership in order to combine strengths, improve areas of weakness, neutralize various threats, or create a means to pursue unique opportunities. Every strategic partnership begins with an interest by one or more parties. When embarking on any new strategic partnership initiative, understanding how the potential partner thinks and what motivates them, allows targeted and productive interest generation strategies to be implemented. Think about how you can customize the seven generic interest generation strategies to create, maintain, or strengthen strategic partner relationships.

Staff

Business Logic. Businesses offer various incentives to attract and retain the staff that their organization needs. This can include higher than normal salaries, flexible work schedules, competitive bonus packages, attractive insurance plans, a unique workplace environment, career growth opportunities, and a host of other perks. Having the right team is crucial for a business to be able to provide the type of value that will set it apart from the competition.

Ministry Logic. Like businesses, Christian ministries can utilize interest generation strategies to attract and retain talented staff members. Once ministries have the right employees in roles where they excel, it is important to think about how to keep them interested, motivated, and productive. Additionally, for a ministry to operate at its best and create as many service opportunities as possible, staff members must understand how to customize the seven generic interest generation strategies within each of the contexts they work in.

Having a thorough understanding of the interest generation principle helps position any ministry to maximize the quantity of opportunities it can create to serve and partner with others. It doesn't guarantee that the desired results will be achieved, but it does *create the opportunity* for the result to be achieved. Accomplishing goals is a process, and generating interest is a critical step in that process.

Visualize

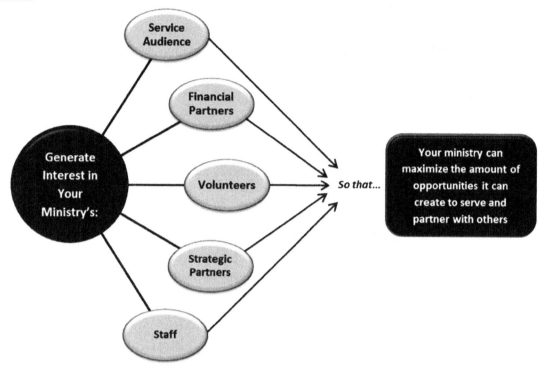

The *Why* Chain

A smart ministry understands the importance of generating interest in the people it desires to influence.

- Why?
    - o Interest generation creates new service and partnership opportunities.
- Why?
    - o Interest is what attracts people to want to learn more about your ministry as well as how to personally get involved.

Rhyme *for* Reason

❖ *Generating interest*
❖ *Creates opportunities anew,*
❖ *Motivating others to learn more*
❖ *About God, your ministry, and you.*

❖ *For your ministry to develop*
❖ *And honor God as you desire,*

> ❖ *Use interest generation*
> ❖ *As a spark to start the fire.*

Scriptural Application

<u>Bible Verse</u>

John 6:2 – "And a great crowd of people followed him because they saw the signs he had performed by healing the sick."

<u>Commentary</u>

When people see, read, or hear about things that interest them, it compels them to want to learn more. Jesus knew that the signs He performed would not only validate His credibility and authority, but that they would create a following of people who wanted to learn more about Him. In John 6:2, we see a large crowd following Jesus. These followers wanted to know why He was doing what He did, how He was able to do it, and what He was going to do next. Jesus wasn't out to seek man's approval, but He did want to draw multitudes of people to His salvation message.

*See pages 188-192 for "Action Questions" related to this principle.

CHAPTER 9

Creating Urgency

"A higher rate of urgency does not imply ever-present panic, anxiety, or fear. It means a state in which complacency is virtually absent." — John P. Kotter

The principle of urgency involves creating enough incentive to spur people towards making a decision, usually within a specified time period. You see the concept of urgency every day on TV commercials and advertisements:

- "Buy this product at 50% off. Offer expires in 30 days!"
- "If you call within the next 90 seconds, we'll upgrade your order to Express Shipping!"
- "You get 10 stainless steel spoons, a blender, 74 piece knife set, custom-designed kitchen apron with your initials, and 30 bamboo-microwaveable covers for only $9.99! That's over a $350 value! But call within the next 10 minutes, and we'll double the entire offer!

Okay, the last one is extreme, but you've seen these kinds of messages in many variations. The two key factors of creating urgency are incentive and time. The incentive is a benefit that can only be received if a commitment is made within a specified time period. If people value the benefit enough, they'll act quickly to avoid missing the opportunity.

Tom Vande Guchte, CEO of Storr Office Environments, understands the value of this principle within his business as he describes below:

> *Creating urgency is about motivating others to take action. Storr is similar to most businesses in that we create programs and a culture that are designed to create urgency for both our clients and for our team members. For our clients, we attempt to motivate them to take action by providing cost-effective solutions, being responsive, leveraging our expertise, and properly setting expectations. All of this is done with the goal of minimizing client risk. Most of our projects require a total workspace makeover, so there is significant cost of downtime and inefficiency if the project is not executed effectively. Showing our client the methodology of how we execute gives them a higher confidence to want to act quickly to accomplish their goals.*

We create urgency for our team members by setting goals, publishing results internally, holding people accountable, and by creating compensation plans that reward results and high performance. Approximately 25% of Storr's overall compensation each year is variable and based on performance. The office furnishings industry is a mature industry with more supply than demand, which has created a very competitive environment with very thin profit margins. Creating urgency is critical to Storr's success—both in the pursuit of clients and in maintaining a culture of continuous improvement.

This principle is an essential component to the positive development of any business or ministry. The key is to use it to create a productive work environment where incentives are the driving factors.

Like businesses, Christian ministries need to understand how to create urgency in others, and equally as important, how to operate with it. Below are two urgency creation tips that can help your ministry create urgency within each of its Five Key Contexts. These are general strategies, so you will need to determine how to customize them in order to maximize their value:

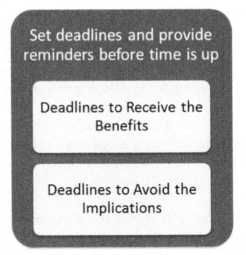

David Johnson, Executive Director of Doulos Partners, leads his ministry with a high sense of urgency and the results are evident in their strategic planning, operations, and ministry culture. Reflecting upon the value of this principle within his ministry, Mr. Johnson said the following:

Watching the "Worldometers" current world population clock is one of the greatest ways that we keep our focus sharp and our foot on the gas of our vision. There are two people dying every second in the world, the majority of which have never heard the name of Jesus. This year alone, there will be an additional 80 million people born in the world, most of who will be raised in a non-Christian home. These statistics keep us charging forward on our mission.

People's eternal destiny literally hangs in the balance. Every day that passes by, the reality of the end of time draws closer. We as a ministry must operate every day as if the world, as we know it, will end tomorrow. If we do, then we will make decisions today in light of that possibility.

God never intended for us to work as mavericks! His plan is always for us to include others. He is teaching us that we are to work like it is up to us, but live like it is totally up to Him. Doulos Partners works extremely hard to inspire people to take action by sharing the needs, statistics, and compelling stories from the field and then trusting the work of the Holy Spirit to bring the partners.

The heartbeat of every ministry should be to create urgency. It is the fuel that causes sustainability and growth. May we live with and lead others to operate with a high sense of urgency. If we do, lives will be changed!

Creating urgency through incentives and deadlines will enable your ministry to accomplish more in less time within each of its Five Key Contexts.

Service Audience

Business Logic. Sales and marketing strategies often include special promotions that are meant to increase the likelihood of generating sales. While some offers are presented through tacky infomercials, the essence of the strategy is the same—to provide the customer with incentives such as reduced costs or bundled packages that can only be received by purchasing within a specific time period. Businesses utilize these strategies in order to expedite sales, and most of the time, it proves effective. The question can then become: "Why not have urgency creation strategies in place all of the time?" The answer is simple: special incentives are only "special" if the receiver believes they are getting additional value beyond the "base offer." If special deals were offered 100% of the time, they would then become base offers and additional incentives would be necessary in order to create the type of customer buying urgency that was originally intended.

While creating urgency is a necessary leadership and management principle, operating with urgency within the context of an organization can pay high dividends. Below is an example from my time at SPS, outlining the importance of creating urgency in others as well as operating with it.

In 2009, SPS gained a new appreciation of what it meant to operate with urgency. We were working with a large IT integrator at the time, and they informed us of a national retailer who was going out of business. Part of the process of closing their stores involved the need for a contractor (SPS) to de-install the IT equipment at each location. Seems simple enough, right? The catch was that the equipment had to be removed at 500 sites (across 41 states) in a single day—all within 10 days of SPS being notified!

After the knee-jerk reaction, our team came together and immediately began planning how to accomplish this monumental task. Initially, we experienced bouts of anxiety, fear, and panic. But after brainstorming and formulating a plan, the negative emotions were quickly replaced with positive thinking, action, and teamwork. We knew that if we deployed the project successfully, there would be extensive value in sharing the story of our success, which would inevitably create more sales opportunities in the future. After an intense week of planning and creating urgency in 150+ field technicians to help us accomplish our objective, we successfully deployed the project and completed all 500 sites within a single day. This wouldn't have been possible without a thorough understanding of this principle.

Ministry Logic. The primary reason why businesses seek to create urgency in the minds of their customers is to increase sales. Ministries can use this principle to increase the amount of opportunities to serve others. If a ministry creates unique value for its service audience(s), it should also have a high sense of urgency to make them aware of that value. When the service audience becomes aware of the value, it should motivate them to want to experience it.

Additionally, if a ministry is structured to solve a problem with significant implications, the ministry will want its service audience to be aware of the implications so that they are incented to seek out the appropriate solutions. This should hold true for every ministry that focuses on evangelism because there isn't a more urgent message than the free gift of salvation through faith in Jesus.

In some cases, a ministry's service audience may be helpless (like those suffering from the aftermath of a natural disaster), so the service audience will have to rely upon the urgency of the ministry itself to take action. Here is one such example, in a statement provided by Ron Wilcox, COO of Samaritan's Purse:

The work of Samaritan's Purse is fundamentally disaster relief on a global scale. This is predicated upon our ability to respond within hours to a disaster and communicate the urgency of the situation to others. When a 7.8 magnitude earthquake hit Nepal in April 2015, Samaritan's Purse quickly deployed over 40 people and sent 700 tons of supplies to meet the urgent needs of food, clean water, medical care, and shelter. In the following weeks, we focused our efforts on providing blankets and shelter with a goal of reaching 50,000 households with these basic necessities to protect them from the imminent rainy season.

While our team and other organizations could not save the thousands that lost their lives during the earthquake itself, our immediate and overwhelming response assuredly saved the lives of thousands more. As with all of our emergency responses, we were very intentional about communicating the urgency of the situation and the importance of an immediate response. Within hours, we sent out an emergency alert email to all of our donors and began to cover our response heavily through our social media channels. We also launched an effort to reach out to news media to spread the word as quickly as possible. God used these efforts to work in the hearts of our donors, volunteers, and others who generously supported our effort and made the work possible.

Every time Samaritan's Purse responds to urgent needs, our focus is not only on solving physical problems, but on delivering the most urgent message of all, the Gospel of the Lord Jesus Christ. There is nothing more valuable than the message that Jesus sacrificed Himself so that our sins could be forgiven and our relationship with God restored. As an organization, we can relieve physical suffering, but eternal hope can only come from making a decision to follow Christ.

Living Water International is a ministry that uses this principle to serve the millions of people around the world who are without access to clean water and/or the Gospel. Jonathan Wiles, VP for Program Excellence with Living Water International, describes the importance of this principle to his ministry and to the people it serves:

The mission that compels us to help communities acquire access to safe water and to experience living water (a personal relationship with Jesus) carries a palpable sense of urgency. The cost of not responding is high: adequately addressing water access, sanitation, and hygiene would prevent the deaths of 260,000 children under the age of five every year. The upside is huge: for every dollar invested in water and sanitation access, communities see more than $4 in economic benefit.[21] The solutions aren't rocket science: simple technologies and approaches for water, sanitation, and hygiene are proven and affordable. This also creates an abundance of opportunities to evangelize, disciple, and build long-term relationships.

Counter-intuitively, we have to guard ourselves against letting our sense of urgency rush us. Hurried, simplistic, cookie-cutter solutions will not achieve lasting benefits. They won't ultimately improve the physical and spiritual health of communities, churches, and families—they may leave them worse off than before. The urgency we feel is ultimately wrapped in our dependence on God and our realization that we are not asking for His blessing on our plan—we are participating in His—which usually involves customizing our approach to most effectively serve others.

---

[21] UN-Water (2014) Global Assessment of Sanitation and Drinking-Water: http://www.who.int/water_sanitation_health/glaas/en

> *When placed under God's authority and direction, this principle can benefit every Christian ministry by maximizing the good works it can do in Jesus' name.*

Think about how your ministry can customize and utilize the urgency creation tips in order to increase outreach opportunities as well as mobilize additional partners to support your efforts.

Financial Partners

Business Logic. Depending on the type of investment opportunity, strategies to create investor urgency can be very effective in helping a business secure an investment quickly. Business investors, and people in general, often procrastinate longer than necessary unless they are incented by special offers and/or strict deadlines. When investors are provided with investment information, a scheduled timeline of when monetary and non-monetary commitments are needed by is included. An incentive for meeting non-monetary deadlines might be avoiding disqualification from future investment discussions. An incentive for meeting monetary deadlines might be the opportunity to receive lower share/stock prices for the same equity value.

Ministry Logic. Most ministries experience a constant need for funding in order to successfully operate. With that being said, creating a sense of urgency in the minds of financial partners is essential to maximizing the likelihood of raising the required funds. Think about how you can customize and utilize the urgency creation tips based on your fundraising needs.

Volunteers

Business Logic. In such a fast-paced world, businesses depend on suppliers that work with a high sense of urgency when responding to and fulfilling their needs. Suppliers that are quick to respond to customer inquiries set themselves apart from their competition and increase the quantity of sales opportunities. Every business wants to work with suppliers that operate with urgency because it shows that the supplier truly cares about helping the business be successful.

Ministry Logic. Whether a ministry needs future volunteers or if emergency needs arise, how you communicate with your volunteers determines how much urgency will be created in them to take action. Volunteers will be motivated to commit their time based on the positive outcomes and/or avoided operational risks that result from their service. To increase the urgency of securing volunteer commitments, set clear and strict deadlines, while providing incremental reminders as deadlines approach. Think about how you can customize and utilize the urgency creation tips to increase the urgency volunteers have in committing their time to your ministry.

Strategic Partners

Business Logic. Strategic partners should be incented to work together because the faster they collaborate, the sooner they can offer added benefits to their customers, investors, staff, and more. If urgency is lacking from either party, re-examining all of the motivations for creating the strategic partnership as well as re-examining the window of time to act, can balance the levels of urgency.

Ministry Logic. Two separate ministries may identify specific needs of a service audience that can only be solved within a limited window of time. By forming a strategic partnership, the ministries will position themselves to serve the audience within the specified time period so that the desired results are achieved. In a strategic partnership context, one of the most important factors in creating urgency that leads to action is agreement. If both parties do not agree on the purpose of the strategic partnership or on the impacts it can make, then the ministry efforts will be unsuccessful. Commit to agreeing with your strategic partners on the goals, strategies, and desired results so that joint objectives are implemented as efficiently and effectively as possible. Think about how you can customize and utilize the urgency creation tips to expedite the creation of new strategic partnerships as well as further develop those that are already established.

Staff

Business Logic. The urgency at which a business's staff operates dictates the operational urgency across every part of the organization. As expressed in the quote from John P. Kotter at the beginning of the chapter, operating with urgency does not mean that everyone is working in a state of fear or panic. Operating with urgency means that forward movement is the goal and complacency is non-existent. Some people are wired with a high sense of urgency while others need to be incented—this is why companies provide unique and attractive incentive plans to maximize employee commitment and results.

Ministry Logic. Operating with a daily sense of urgency does not (and should not) mean that there is a fear of God not working in your ministry. In truth, God is always working. Because of this, your response should be a commitment to operating with a high sense of action-oriented urgency while trusting Him with the results. Think about how you can customize and utilize the urgency creation tips so that your ministry's staff can accomplish more in less time.

We walk the tight-rope of eternity every day. We tend to pace ourselves with what God has called us to do, based on the assumption that we have a long-life ahead of us. I am guilty of this myself. Think back to the first pages of this book and St. Augustine's quote: "Pray as if everything depends on God. Work as if everything depends on you." Value the time you are given, use it wisely, and value the time of others. Don't put off until tomorrow what can be done today. Create more value for your ministry by operating with productive, God-honoring urgency.

Visualize

The curve in the diagram below shows the probability of commitments based on the two main factors of creating urgency: incentive and time. When incentive is high and the allotted time to act is low, the probability of a commitment is high. When incentive is low and allotted time to act is high, the probability of making a commitment is low.

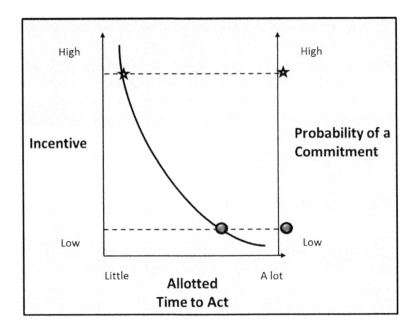

The *Why* Chain

A smart ministry understands the importance of creating and operating with urgency.

- Why?
  - o Creating urgency reduces the time it takes for decisions to be made.
- Why?
  - o People tend to procrastinate on making decisions or achieving results, if incentives and/or deadlines are not in place.

Rhyme *for* Reason

❖ *Do you live like you have forever*
❖ *To make decisions and implement plans?*
❖ *Or do you live like you are dying*
❖ *To maximize the workings of your hands?*

❖ *Christians should live with urgency,*
❖ *And your ministry should do the same*
❖ *Doing good works that aren't just temporal,*
❖ *But that will eternally remain.*

❖ *Learn to operate with urgency*
❖ *In everything that you do,*
❖ *Honoring God with your work*
❖ *To increase what He can do through you.*

Scriptural Application

<u>Bible Verse</u>

Matthew 3:2 – "And saying, 'Repent, for the kingdom of heaven has come near.'"

<u>Commentary</u>

Matthew 3:2 as well as other verses in the Gospels speak to the urgency of placing our faith in Jesus. No one understands the reason for this urgency better than Christ. While we don't see it in its truest form, the implications of our sin are bigger than we can imagine and the hatred that the devil has for us is more than our minds can conceive. Jesus, not being bound by sin, time, or space, has an eternal perspective on the spiritual forces we are up against, and He knows that we are helpless without Him. In addition, Jesus also knows the benefits that await those who place their trust in Him and live their life according to His will. Francis Chan responds to Jesus' words this way: "When I read the statements of Christ, there seems to be this urgency and intensity. I guess that's what I get out of it when I read the tone of the Scriptures, which is very different from the tone of our culture."

See pages 193-195 for "Action Questions" related to this principle.

CHAPTER 10

Handling Objections

"An objection is not a rejection; it is simply a request for more information." — *Bo Bennett*

Objections are either valid or invalid statements that are a response to something a person has read, seen, or heard. Valid objections are true statements and they provide organizations with the opportunity to improve based on the feedback and insight from others. Invalid objections are untrue statements generated from false information or misperceptions. Invalid objections require organizations to respond to the objector with factual information in an effort to clarify the truth so that the objection is no longer in question. Properly handling valid and invalid objections is essential for every business and ministry that desires to continuously improve and help others make well-informed decisions.

Businesses face objections every day and there are two ways to handle them: proactively or reactively. Some businesses choose to proactively address common objections that customers, investors, suppliers, or staff members may have. They do this through publically available FAQ's (frequently asked questions) or through various marketing material. From a reactive standpoint, businesses respond to objections that are uncommon or not anticipated. In these situations, objectors may be confused, angry, or have a sincere desire to learn more. Whatever the case, the business must be ready to provide an appropriate and timely response.

James Forrest, Founder of Forrest Firm, understands the value of properly handling objections in his business and in any organizational setting:

> *Law firms face some pretty common objections. You can either be insulted by these objections, or you can take them to heart and improve. When we launched Forrest Firm, we designed our business model as a response to the validity of those objections. Business executives find the costs of legal services to be excessive and surprising, so we came up with several billing packages based on our client's legal needs, budgets, and cash flow cycles. To keep our pricing competitive, we have come up with creative staffing and corporate real estate models to keep our overhead low. We heard time and again that attorneys and their support staff were too slow to respond to calls, emails, and meeting requests, often resulting in missed business opportunities. Because of this, we committed to faster response times of 24-48 hours, depending upon the nature of the request, to*

adapt our law firm to the speed of modern business. The two-minute video on our web-site is a great example of how we proactively address common objections that our prospective clients have.

Since we have taken a proactive, transparent stance to the most common objections our clients may have regarding doing business with a law firm—and the fact that we agree with them—we have been able to build trust quicker and align our relationships in ways that are mutually beneficial to all parties. Being able to properly handle objections is a critical principle for any organization—it creates trust and removes doubts and fears.

Below is a simple process that can be used in situations where valid objections are presented:

Like in business, your ministry must be aware that objections will be present across all of its Five Key Contexts. Your ministry will face valid objections, which will create opportunities for improvement based on the insight and perspectives of others. Your ministry will also face invalid objections, which will create opportunities to clarify why they are untrue or inaccurate. Whatever the situation, objections will always be present, so it is crucial to understand how to properly address them.

The following outlines how Southland Christian Church utilizes this principle within its ministry, as described by Lead Executive Pastor, Chris Hahn:

Southland Christian Church functions openly, meaning we respond to every criticism with an open heart and mind, taking an empathetic approach toward other people's feelings and views. There have been many instances where we have learned from "valid" objections. The unique perspectives and feedback we receive from others has proven to be extremely valuable to the growth and development of our ministry. We have also received many "invalid" objections. We invite open dialogue and are completely comfortable in those situations. Open dialogue gives us the opportunity to learn and an opportunity to educate. We always promote a culture of question asking and objection sharing in healthy ways.

Southland has hosted Q gatherings where we openly take any question in a live room that people want to ask. We capture the Q sessions on video and post them on our website in order to be helpful for others. We've had weekends where we've opened up Twitter or texting opportunities for worship participants to pose questions—then, in the middle of the worship experience, we answer them. These engagements always promote follow up conversations that give us opportunity to listen well and to share well so that rumors are dispelled and people are clear on the whys and hows of what we do.

When preaching the Word of God to a large audience, there will always be people that object to things for various reasons. Practically speaking, anytime people are involved in anything, there's the opportunity for disagreements and objections to arise. Southland is always pursuing harmony, but we are bold about ensuring that the truth is proclaimed in minor issues as well as in regards to God's Word. Christian ministries should understand how to properly handle objections so that their credibility and opportunities for positive development will not be jeopardized.

Similar to the process above, the process below can be used when handling invalid objections:

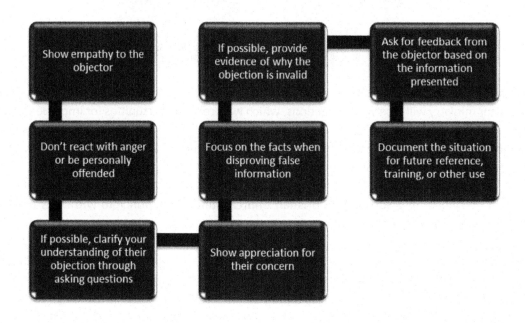

Having the ability to properly handle objections will benefit every Christian ministry within each of its Five Key Contexts.

Service Audience

Business Logic. The most common context in which businesses face objections is from customers, especially prospective customers. Today, we live in a world where people's time and attention spans are limited, so new offers are often prematurely dismissed, even if the business's value proposition provides legitimate value. This is where interest generation strategies are essential as they are designed to help businesses pique a prospective customer's interest enough to gain their time and attention. If the business does this successfully, the prospective customer will likely have valid and invalid objections about what is being offered, and the business will have to respond accordingly.

The following outlines one of many experiences I've had at eWater in regard to properly handling customer objections:

> In 2014, eWater launched a new offer and as a result, there were numerous valid and invalid objections from prospective customers. In most cases, the invalid objections stemmed from the customer's lack of understanding. In one instance, a prospect told me they weren't interested in a particular eWater product because they believed it had a short shelf life. In truth, the product in question had a shelf life of well over a month. I previously shared this information with them numerous times, but they still came to a false conclusion—an invalid objection. Fortunately, I was able to re-present the value of our offer and clarify the product's shelf life, resulting in the customer making a purchase decision days later.

> eWater has experienced many valid objections as well from those internal and external to our organization. With any new company, lessons are learned on a daily basis, frequently through the feedback and perspectives from others. Insights from customers, employees, investors, suppliers, and strategic partners have helped eWater innovate and improve, which has helped us create new capabilities, refine our plans, and position our company for success.

Ministry Logic. Christian ministries will face many valid and invalid objections based on who their service audience is. As an example: compare a service audience that financially contributes to a ministry (such as church members) to a service audience that does not. Because church members directly help the church operate via tithes and offerings, members will be more vocal in expressing their objections and opinions about various topics. Contributing money gives people a sense of ownership, as well as a platform for their voice to be heard. Because of this, a service audience that does not financially contribute to a ministry will likely voice fewer objections. In such cases, the ministry should invite them to raise their objections, as some may be valid, which can lead to innovation in numerous areas.

Lead Pastor of Cedar Creek Church, Lee Powell, has experience with handling both valid and invalid objections. The following statement includes a story describing an invalid objection raised by various Cedar Creek church members after a Christmas Eve service years ago:

> *It was John Lydgate who once said, "You can please some of the people all of the time, you can please all of the people some of the time, but you can't please all of the people all of the time." Good leaders know that pleasing everyone isn't practical. However, the key is to be a good listener with those who aren't supportive.*
>
> *Cedar Creek operates on a "5-Agreements" ministry philosophy (three of which we learned of from Lifechurch.tv):*
>
> 1. *We will do anything short of sin to reach lost people.*
> 2. *We agree that the cause of the church is the Greatest Cause on the planet.*
> 3. *We agree that the church can never get too big!*
> 4. *We agree to be an example of Jesus' Love behind and beyond the walls of our church.*
> 5. *We agree to do more with less.*
>
> *This ministry philosophy serves as an aid for us when receiving or responding to objections people have about our ministry. When we receive valid objections that are aligned with our beliefs and ministry philosophy, we act upon them and improve as an organization. When objections arise that have no biblical truth and counter our ministry philosophy, we do our best to educate the dissenter and in some cases succeed in helping them see their error. In other cases, we have found that our church may not be the right fit for some. Here's a quick story of one such case:*
>
>> *A couple of years ago, we decided to use overturned garbage cans to help make music at our Christmas Eve services. 95% of the audience loved it. However, a small group of "Creekers" thought it was in poor taste. Some of the concerned talked to me personally—others wrote to me afterwards. The result of our Christmas Eve services were 1,200 lost souls giving their lives to Jesus! The unconventional method of our Christmas Eve services helped create the opportunity to share the Gospel with non-believers. For the people that thought we were out of line, I attempted to educate them on why we did what we did. I kindly told them that if they were more concerned about personal preferences than about Cedar Creek reaching lost souls, they were at the wrong church.*

Every Christian ministry's ultimate goal should be to do their part in helping fulfill the Great Commission. Properly handling objections is an important principle to understand along that journey.

Financial Partners

Business Logic. Businesses hear objections from investors throughout various stages before or after an investment is made. This is true whether the investor is highly knowledgeable about what the business offers or if they have no prior knowledge. When deciding whether to invest, investors will have valid and invalid objections concerning the business's market intelligence, competitive awareness, competitive advantages, company valuation, price per equity share, estimated ROI timeline, and more. An experienced business can proactively address common objections, enabling it to focus on responding to unforeseen objections. As mentioned above, there are numerous valid and invalid reasons why an investor might object. However, it is the manner in which a business can address the objections that will influence the probability of securing an investment.

Ministry Logic. For ministries, being able to properly handle objections is essential in the financial partner context because at some point, raising funds will depend on how well objections are addressed. Financial partners are similar to business investors, in that when it's time to contribute their funds, hesitation can set in. You can combat this natural human tendency through knowledge, empathy, and wisdom, by proactively addressing known/common objections. Also, provide financial partners with opportunities to object to your request(s), so that you can improve from their valid objections and properly address invalid objections. No financial partner wants to feel like there is a hidden agenda regarding how funds will be used, so think about how to be as transparent as possible with the following information:

- Why their money is needed.
- What it is needed for.
- When it is needed.
- Who will be impacted.
- When they will be impacted.
- The results that can be expected.
- The results that are achieved.

Volunteers

Business Logic. Generally speaking, businesses work with suppliers because suppliers have capabilities or expertise that the business needs but doesn't have on staff. Because of this, businesses need suppliers that can add value to their plans. A business may have a goal of what it wants to achieve, and utilizes suppliers to help execute its plans. Valuable suppliers may see flaws in the business's plans (valid objections), which will help the business avoid mistakes and unnecessary costs. On the other hand, businesses also need suppliers that are humble when they disagree with what a business is requesting of them.

If the disagreement is an invalid objection, the supplier must recognize their error and move forward with humility.

Ministry Logic. Your ministry's volunteers may incrementally express valid or invalid objections. Their objections may relate to the purpose of a project, confusion over a role, a past experience, and more. Give your volunteers the opportunity to question the plans they are part of. You may find that their valid objections lead to improved ways of doing things. When presented with invalid objections, you will have the opportunity to alleviate their concerns. Treat every volunteer objection with the same care as if it came from your service audience—you never know how a single idea might positively impact your ministry.

Strategic Partners

Business Logic. Any time someone is attempting to influence another person or organization, the opportunity for objections will arise. In the strategic partner context, one or both parties evaluating the partnership opportunity will likely have objections. Since strategic partnerships are highly intimate business relationships, it is important for each organization to have a "partnership mindset" when working through concerns. A common objection can be concern over the profit sharing structure. Strategic planning and vision casting create excitement, but when profit sharing and money allocation are discussed, reality hits. When businesses begin to see how finances will be allocated, it creates an environment for objections to arise. Some objections may be valid, which can change the terms of the strategic partnership. Others may be invalid, and in such instances, the businesses must then decide how committed they are to working through them together.

Ministry Logic. If your ministry desires to establish a strategic partnership, this may involve presenting your vision, mission, and strategy for the partnership in order to captivate the other party's interest. After presenting the why, what, and how of the partnership, don't expect the prospective partner to be "all in" immediately. It's natural to assume that others will think similarly to you, but in many cases they won't, and that is where objections will arise. Some of these objections may be valid and will help refine the purpose and direction of the strategic partnership. Other objections may be invalid, due to a lack of understanding of certain terms or objectives. Whatever the case, ministries that partner together must work through objections with mutual respect for each other.

Staff

Business logic. Staff members are responsible for addressing nearly every objection a business receives. This is one of many reasons why every staff member should be as knowledgeable as possible about the business. In regard to organizational innovation, some of the most valuable staff members are ones that question the status quo and challenge the business with better ways of doing things. Sometimes these types of objections are invalid, but in instances where they prove valid, they can trigger innovation and idea creation to help the business improve.

Ministry Logic. Equipping your staff to handle objections will help them fulfill their job responsibilities with as much knowledge and confidence as possible. Since "practice makes perfect," consider creating practice scenarios through role-play. Play the role of an apprehensive financial partner, an inquisitive volunteer, an angry member within your service audience, or a concerned strategic partner. Practice how to respond to valid and invalid objections proactively and reactively. In addition, give staff members the opportunity to generate ideas and question your ministry's current way of operating—this will create a culture of continuous improvement and organizational innovation.

Visualize

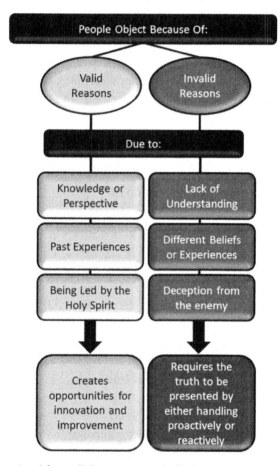

Inspired from *"The Brain Audit,"*[22] by Sean D'Souza

---

[22] Sean D'Souza, *The Brain Audit: Why Customers Buy (And Why They Don't)* (Auckland, New Zealand: Psychotactics Ltd., 2009), 77.

The *Why* Chain

A smart ministry understands the importance of properly handling *valid* objections.

- Why?
    - o Through the knowledge and perspectives of others, valid objections help ministries improve.
- Why?
    - o It can be difficult for ministries to identify operational weaknesses when immersed in daily tasks and responsibilities.
- Why?
    - o A third-party perspective is sometimes necessary to identify opportunities for innovation.

A smart ministry understands the importance of properly handling *invalid* objections.

- Why?
    - o Invalid objections are not based upon truth or reality.
- Why?
    - o People may lack understanding for numerous reasons so it is critical for ministries to successfully disprove invalid objections.
- Why?
    - o Overcoming invalid objections, and presenting facts and truth, enables well-informed decisions to be made.

Rhyme *for* Reason

- ❖ *Most people tend to object*
- ❖ *To what is different, unique, or new.*
- ❖ *They can be slow to believe and trust*
- ❖ *Not knowing what is true.*

- ❖ *Objections that are valid*
- ❖ *Create opportunities to improve.*
- ❖ *And objections that are not*
- ❖ *Should quickly be disproved.*

Scriptural Application

<u>Bible Verse</u>

John 20:27 – "Then he said to Thomas, 'Put your finger here; see my hands. Reach out your hand and put it into my side. Stop doubting and believe.'"

<u>Commentary</u>

Jesus faced and disproved objections throughout the entire course of His public ministry. Objections came from the opposition, religious leaders, those earnestly seeking the truth, and even from His own followers. Some objections came in the form of antagonistic questions, with the intent of leading Jesus into a trap. Other objections were rooted in people's sincere desire to understand who Jesus was. In the case of the disciple Thomas, Jesus spoke truth into His doubts. Jesus wasn't angry with Thomas and was likely empathetic towards him. Jesus can handle our doubts as well and it is His desire to reveal the truth to us through the Bible and the Holy Spirit.

*See pages 196-198 for "Action Questions" related to this principle.

CHAPTER 11

Leveraging Testimonials

"There is much more credibility in the words of other unbiased people than in your own words of self-promotion." — Kim Harrison, Cutting Edge PR

In today's world, people are skeptical about virtually everything. Society is becoming more cynical, and this cynicism is present in nearly every business context. Why have people become so non-trusting? From a business perspective, the primary contributing factor stems from purchases that have failed to meet expectations—the product didn't work, the seller provided poor customer service, hidden costs were exposed only after the purchase was made, etc. As negative experiences continue to occur over time, customers begin to doubt the deals they are being offered. With that being said, how do businesses overcome this skepticism to successfully generate sales?

One of the best ways for a business to validate the credibility of its offers is by leveraging third-party testimonials from non-biased, trustworthy people and organizations. A credible third-party testimonial endorses the offer as one that can be trusted. No other testimonial is more influential in the sales process than those from satisfied customers. Sharing the positive experiences of those who have purchased before, gives prospective customers the confidence to make intelligent buying decisions.

New businesses, as well as existing businesses with new offers, frequently partner with "early adopters"— people who match the targeted customer profile and are willing to test the product or service to provide feedback. Early adopters are provided with special terms of use that bare them no risk or obligation. If they have a positive experience, the business will utilize their testimonials in strategic marketing and sales efforts. The true test of an offer's viability, however, comes from satisfied customers who don't receive special pricing or terms. If the standard offer yields positive testimonials from paying customers, the business has proof that the offer is valuable and unique.

Businesses and ministries can leverage two types of testimonials in order to create trust in those they are trying to influence. The first is an all-out-positive testimonial, in which someone communicates how wonderful their experience was. The second is a testimonial that author Sean D'Souza refers to in his book, *The Brain Audit*, as a "reverse testimonial."[23] In a reverse testimonial, the testimonial begins with an initial objection, but ends with a positive experience, proving the objection to be invalid. Both types of testimonials are effective. However, the latter can be a more strategic way to overcome skepticisms that many people have.

Dave Jones, Co-founder of The Reset Agency, places high value on this principle within his business, as described below:

> *The Reset Agency has a unique process and philosophy that has helped differentiate us from other coaching firms. We make it personal and about the client. While we are delighted to communicate the value we can offer to individuals and organizations, it speaks higher volumes when the people we have served can share their own stories about the impact our company has had on them. When we meet with people over lunch or dinner and share with them the success stories of those The Reset Agency has helped in the past, it motivates them to want to take action. When prospective clients view the testimonies listed on our website, they gain a better appreciation of the fact that our goal is to exceed their expectations. Success stories help others see that problems are temporary, solutions are around the corner, and that hope exists in every circumstance. Every business and ministry should exist to change people's lives for the better. No one can argue with changed lives, and it's these kinds of stories that are never forgotten.*

Key indicators of a ministry's impact are the quantity and quality of testimonials it generates. Kyle Philips, USA Director of International Leadership Institute, describes the value of this principle to his ministry:

> *The formal communication policy from the ILI office to its staff is "lead with stories." ILI constantly works to tell the stories of people who have been impacted by its training throughout the global network. Through Facebook, Instagram, and other familiar social media venues, ILI alumni share what is going on, ask for prayer, and celebrate what the Lord is doing. Vimeo video clips of people telling stories are regularly captured and then embedded into email blasts on the ILITeam.org website. Additionally, a full color news-letter goes to our financial partners quarterly, encouraging them with accounts of what the Lord is doing through faithful leaders serving in the global ILI network.*
>
> *ILI has published a coffee table book entitled, Changing Lives. It tells the stories of twen-ty-five faithful people who are living very different lives because they have become "leaders equipping leaders." Changing Lives has become a tool alumni can use to help people understand the impact of ILI.*

---

[23] Sean D'Souza, *The Brain Audit: Why Customers Buy (And Why They Don't)* (Auckland, New Zealand: Psychotactics Ltd., 2009), 87.

Through ILI's podcast, ILITeamTalk.com, I invite those who have come alive to God's Kingdom to call and share their stories of what God has done in them and through them. For example, one businessman from California's Central Valley has circled the globe speaking into the lives of leaders in Africa, Latin America, and Asia through ILI's global network. While he is not especially gifted or educated for "ministry," he is simply faithful and has become equipped through ILI's training. As others hear his story, they come to realize that they too can be used by God to do great things beyond their imagining.

People come alive when they tap into God's heart for the lost and realize that He calls all believers, not just the professional clergy, "to do far more abundantly than all we ask or think." Nothing removes doubts, fears, or skepticism like hearing the stories of others who have been changed.

All-out-positive testimonials and reverse testimonials are effective ways of sharing experiences to motivate others to take action. Either type of testimonial can positively impact your ministry within each of its Five Key Contexts.

Service Audience

Business Logic. As previously discussed, the short-term goal of many start-up companies is to bring on "early adopters" to generate testimonials, establish credibility, and create momentum in their target markets. In time, if a business secures a solid and growing list of testimonials, its selling strategies will change. Prior to having positive testimonials, a business has no choice but to focus marketing and selling efforts on the attributes of its products or services. After customer testimonials are generated, the focus shifts to sharing the positive experiences of satisfied customers—a strategy called testimonial based selling.

My experience at eWater Advantage has given me an immense appreciation for the value of this principle. In many cases, our new customer relationships are directly linked to positive testimonials generated from past customers and other credible sources.

If you haven't heard of engineered water before, being told that it 1) kills germs more effectively than chemicals, 2) is safe enough to swallow, and 3) costs less than conventional cleaning methods, is something people in our industry refer to as "snake-oil"—a term that means "too good to be true." eWater's solutions, however, are proven and backed by science. To help gain credibility within our target markets, we leverage the value of testimonials generated from:

1. *Our current customers, to ensure that prospective customers don't perceive working with us as a risk.*
2. *Subject matter experts, to ensure that non-biased professionals support the claims we make about our solutions.*

3. *The success of other engineered water companies, because as the saying goes,
    "A rising tide lifts all boats." Since this technology is still relatively new in the U.S.,
    hearing that others are succeeding helps the credibility of eWater's offering.*

Whether a product is a commodity or a high-tech solution, most customers want to know that others have gone before them and were satisfied with their experience. The majority of the time, customers are hesitant to try something that no one else has tried before. They fear losing money, wasting time, or taking a risk that may negatively affect their business or personal life. There is fear in the unknown, and testimonials from satisfied customers help to remove this fear. Strong testimonials can also decrease customer price sensitivity. As an example, without assurance that other customers have been satisfied with their purchase, a $500 product may be perceived as too expensive. However, the $500 may seem reasonable or attractive if customer testimonials justify the price for the value received. In many product and service categories, the majority of a customer's buying criteria is based on the experiences of past customers.

Tom Vande Guchte, CEO of Storr Office Environments, shared the following statement regarding the power of this principle within his business:

> *Storr serves clients all over the US in commercial markets including Education, Healthcare, Small Businesses, and more. The true test of the success of any project is the satisfaction of our client. Storr has been measuring client satisfaction for over 15 years, and over the past four years, Storr has an average client satisfaction score of 9.0 out of 10 and a "net promoter" score of 76%. We have committed ourselves to capturing positive client experiences through printed testimonials, in-depth case studies, and video recordings. Prospective clients, investors, suppliers, or potential new hires can visit our website to learn about the types of projects we've implemented and the customer feedback we've received.*

> *We also share these stories with our team members to help us create a culture of excellence, serving, winning, and client satisfaction. While many of our new customers are acquired through outbound sales, large portions are also acquired from the testimonials and referrals of current or past clients. We believe there is no better way for an organization to show its credibility than through sharing the positive testimonials it receives from others.*

Ministry Logic. There may be no better method of developing trust with new members of your service audience than by sharing positive testimonials from those your ministry has already impacted. Prospective service audience members are likely experiencing the same circumstances of those your ministry has or is already serving. Because of these similarities, sharing the experiences of those who have been positively impacted by your ministry is one of the most powerful tools at your disposal in order to increase the quantity of outreach opportunities. Use all-out-positive testimonials to demonstrate how your ministry has helped your service audience(s). Use reverse testimonials to show how initial objections and skepticisms were overcome.

Financial Partners

Business Logic. Depending on how long a business has been operating, customer testimonials may or may not be available to share with prospective investors. If they are available, sharing them can be highly beneficial in helping to remove any initial fears or doubts investors may have. If they are not available, here are three ways businesses can still leverage the value of testimonials in investor discussions:

1. The business's leadership team may have a reputation of being successful, hardworking, and honest. Connecting investors with individuals that can share past experiences of working with the leadership team will boost their confidence in regards to *who* they are investing in.
2. The business may have testimonials from third-party references, which will validate the credibility of its vision, mission, strategy, and/or business model. These can include regulatory agencies, industry experts, accreditations, seals of approval, and more. This gives investors a greater sense of confidence in *what* they are investing in.
3. The business may have successful competitors. If so, the business can leverage its competitors' success as a means to validate its plans and lower an investor's perceived risk of investing into "the unknown".

Ministry Logic. Christian ministries can utilize testimonials to increase the confidence that financial partners have in contributing to their ministry. Learning about the positive experiences of others will motivate financial partners to want to invest because they will see and feel the impacts being made before contributing their funds. But what about a ministry that is raising funds for a new initiative? Below are three methods in which testimonials can be created and shared in this scenario.

1. Document conversations with individuals who can share their views on your ministry's financial needs—this includes discussing problems that currently exist as well as positive impacts that can be made if the necessary funding becomes available. Speak with people from all Five Key Contexts to ensure multiple perspectives are presented.
2. Generate testimonials from third-party experts, referencing factual information that supports and validates your vision, mission, strategy, and/or ministry model.
3. Reference success stories from similar ministries. In other words, leverage the success and momentum of those who have already "been there and done that."

Always be on the lookout for ways to gather and promote all-out-positive and reverse testimonials in order to help motivate your financial partners to take action.

Volunteers

Business Logic. When businesses establish new supplier relationships, suppliers are asked to provide customer references to help the business determine the level of risk (or benefit) in establishing the new relationship. On the other hand, suppliers will share stories with their peers regarding what it's like to work with a particular business. If the business has a reputation of treating suppliers poorly, word will travel fast and the business will suffer. If the business has a reputation for treating suppliers as valued partners, suppliers will share their positive experiences and the business will benefit in numerous ways. Credible testimonials have the power to positively influence one or all components of a business's supply chain.

Ministry Logic. Just as a business's suppliers can influence other suppliers, a ministry's current volunteers can influence future volunteers. Below are two examples of volunteer testimonials—one illustrates an all-out positive testimonial and the other a reverse testimonial, each purposed with influencing new volunteers for a future outreach event.

Your ministry is gearing up to launch its 2nd annual summer outreach program. Four months leading up to it, you start promoting the event to create a buzz. Part of your promotional effort includes sharing staff and volunteer testimonials. At a volunteer interest meeting, you show two videos from last year's event. In the first video, the volunteer gives an all-out-positive testimonial:

> *This was the best volunteer experience I've ever had. I formed many new friendships and had a great time interacting with the people we served. I highly recommend this volunteer opportunity to anyone who enjoys serving others in Jesus' name. It was a real blessing, and I hope I have the opportunity to volunteer again next year!*

The volunteer in the second video provides a reverse testimonial, beginning with initial objections and concluding with a positive experience:

> *When I learned of this volunteer opportunity, I was excited but also hesitant to commit. My husband works long hours, so I was concerned about childcare for my 2-year-old since she was not in daycare. I was also nervous about sharing my faith with people I had just met. Upon hearing more about the program, I learned that childcare would be provided onsite by church staff—one of the ladies in my small group was actually part of the childcare team. Additionally, the program leaders were wonderful and I was able to choose which areas I was most comfortable serving in. By the end of the week, I developed a special relationship with a teenager named Cassie, and had the opportunity to lead her to the Lord. I'm really looking forward to next year's program and would encourage anyone who is interested in volunteering to sign up.*

As seen in the examples above, your ministry can utilize testimonials from past volunteers to increase the likelihood of future volunteers committing their time to serve.

Strategic Partners

Business Logic. When businesses are completing the due diligence process prior to forming a strategic partnership, seeking out references or testimonials from others is crucial. Before joining as a single entity, each business will want to ensure they are not overlooking any critical information that could negatively impact the partnership's viability. References can (and should) include previous or current customers, investors, suppliers, and staff members. This feedback will ultimately increase or decrease the desire of each business in pursuing a strategic partnership. Regardless of the outcome, testimonials will help each business make well-informed decisions.

Ministry Logic. Providing testimonials from each of your ministry's Five Key Contexts will support your efforts in forming strategic partnerships. These testimonials will be valuable in ensuring your partner is confident about working with your ministry.

Through its many strategic partnerships around the world, The JESUS Film Project captures and shares personal stories of others to help advance God's Kingdom. Below are three such stories, shared by Josh Newell, Director of Marketing and Communications for The JESUS Film Project:

> *A large part of the effectiveness of The JESUS Film Project comes from sharing the stories of the people that have been impacted by our ministry. Personal testimonies allow us to go well beyond the statistical metrics that gauge our ministry's impact. They put faces, names, and stories behind people who have given their lives to Jesus after viewing or listening to our resources. Here are some examples:*

>> *The JESUS Film Project has partnered with missionaries that took our film, projectors, and power generators into areas that didn't have electricity in order to share the Gospel with people that have never heard it before. In one such instance in South Africa, 350 people viewed the video, most of whom had never previously seen a movie. The missionary leading the trip said, "You could see them physically jump back at the sight of the serpent tempting Jesus. When soldiers whipped Jesus, you could hear grown adults crying." 145 people became followers of Christ that day.*

>> *Some years ago in Peru, communist guerillas stopped a missionary couple traveling to show the film in a village. The guerillas took the projector and reels of the film. Later, one of the guerillas contacted the couple to apologize and tell them he and some of his friends had chosen to follow Christ because of the movie.*

>> *In 2010, when 33 Chilean miners were trapped more than 2,000 feet below the surface for over two months, Campus Crusade for Christ in Chile arranged for*

each of them to receive an MP3 player in the mine with an audio version of the film. Many of them made a personal decision to follow Jesus as a result.

These kinds of stories allow us to advance our mission in significant ways. By sharing salvation stories and personal testimonies, our partners gain a vision for the ease of use and the many different ways our resources can be leveraged. This is a multiplicative effect. The more who get excited and think, "I can do this," leads to more people sharing their faith. This virtuous cycle also is a construct for us to re-tell the creative ways in which people all over the world use our tools, serving as a platform for future creative use. Recruiting, prayer, and donor activities all benefit from compelling stories of how God has used and is using our ministry to help fulfill the Great Commission.

Staff

Business Logic. A business's staff members are responsible for gathering testimonials. In some cases, testimonials are created in raw form, meaning the business receiving the testimonial has no influence on its content. In other cases, a business's employees will assist in the creation of the testimonial. This is done by asking questions and leading others through the process of developing a statement or by writing the testimonial and seeking approval from the person being referenced. Either way, assisting others in writing a testimonial does not diminish its authenticity. If the person being referenced as the author of the testimonial agrees with its content, the testimonial can be used as an authentic source of information to share with others.

Ministry Logic. A ministry's staff members are responsible for gathering testimonials. Similar to businesses, ministries can receive raw testimonials or can assist others in the creation of testimonials to ensure that the statements support the ministry's goals and objectives. As long as the person who is being referenced agrees with the statement, no matter how it's developed, the ministry can use their testimonial as an authentic source to motivate others to take action. That's the whole point of testimonials—showing others that there is more to gain by taking action than by standing still. John F. Kennedy once said, "There are risks and costs to action. But they are far less than the long range risks of comfortable inaction." I agree.

Sharing testimonials may be the most powerful way to mobilize an individual's commitment to your vision or mission. Get them in print. Get them on video. Share them with as many people as you can through as many avenues possible. Tap into people's spirit, heart, and mind by leveraging the positive experiences of others.

Visualize

The *Why* Chain

A smart ministry understands the importance of leveraging testimonials.

- Why?
    - o Testimonials are a powerful way to display the credibility, trustworthiness, and authenticity of your ministry.
- Why?
    - o People place high value on the experiences of those that have gone before them.
- Why?
    - o Most people need validation from others in order to reduce their skepticism about new things.
- Why?
    - o No one wants to regret their decisions. Testimonials create assurance that a decision to take action is the right choice.

Rhyme *for* Reason

- ❖ *Gather the testimonials*
- ❖ *Of those who have gone before,*
- ❖ *To show others the opportunity*
- ❖ *For what God might have in store.*

- ❖ *Whether they focus on the positives*
- ❖ *Or prove how objections are untrue,*
- ❖ *Testimonials will help you achieve*
- ❖ *What God has called your ministry to do.*

Scriptural Application

<u>Bible Verse</u>

Luke 8:39 – "'Return home and tell how much God has done for you.' So the man went away and told all over town how much Jesus had done for him."

<u>Commentary</u>

Luke 8:39 is one of many examples where Jesus demonstrates His understanding and appreciation of testimonials. As Jesus' public ministry was expanding, many people looked upon His works with skepticism and objection. In Luke 8:39, even though the man desired to stay and follow Jesus, He instructed him to return to his hometown and tell others about what He had done. This verse is also a great example of how Jesus trusted His people to bear testimony of His good works.

NOTE – See the book of Acts for numerous "reverse testimonial" examples from the Apostle Paul, showing how he converted from being one of Christianity's greatest enemies in his time, to becoming one of its greatest proponents. Towards the end of Acts, Paul gave his reverse testimony multiple times to top officials in Judea. He spoke of his initial fears and reaction to Christianity and then spoke about how he met Jesus. His testimony was so powerful that even the heathen King Agrippa said, "You almost persuaded me to be a Christian."

*See pages 199-201 for "Action Questions" related to this principle.

CHAPTER 12

Managing Relationships

"Man is a knot into which relationships are tied." — Antoine de Saint-Exupéry

The preceding 11 chapters all have one thing in common—every principle, and all of the contexts in which they can be applied, are meaningless without properly managing relationships. Relationships are the glue that holds every organization together.

Every business is constantly trying to find new ways to create sustainable competitive advantages over its competitors. Businesses with strong internal relationships between staff members and strong external relationships with customers, investors, suppliers, and strategic partners are able to create more value than the competition. Everything is easier when relationships are strong because each party cares about the well-being and success of the other. Conversely, weak relationships can create inefficiencies, stifle growth, and jeopardize the potential for success. Operating a business can sometimes seem so complicated, yet the essence of why it exists is simple. It's all about relationships.

In the following statement, Jim Anthony, Founder of Anthony & Company, communicates the importance of properly managing relationships in his business:

> Anthony & Co. exists to positively impact people's lives and help transform communities. This is accomplished through the relationships we have developed with those we serve, work, and partner with. We help our clients achieve their real estate goals by operating with professionalism and expertise, honoring our commitments, and creating an atmosphere of trust. We reward hard working and dedicated suppliers with our loyalty, through designating them as preferred partners. We treat our co-workers with kindness, compassion, and courtesy and encourage open communication to resolve disputes. We ensure that expectations are clear and adequately equip those who are responsible for fulfilling each task our business requires.
>
> As the leader of our company, it is my responsibility to ensure that the relationships we create reflect the values that govern our organization. Everything belongs to God, and we are placed here to be good stewards of the time and relationships He has blessed us

with. I would strongly advise any business or ministry that wants to do the most they can with what they have to understand the importance of properly managing relationships. It is the foundation upon which all other principles stand.

Similar to the business context, the best word to describe the purpose of operating a ministry is "relationships." As mentioned in chapter three, two categories of relationships drive all ministry efforts: personal relationships with God and with other people. Every relationship can be evaluated and measured based on its quantitative or qualitative attributes. In our personal relationship with God, the relationship is strictly qualitative (not quantitative because there is only one True God). The quality of our relationship with God is based on our desire to know Him, our decisions to be obedient, and our commitment to love Him more than anything else in our lives. Personal relationships with others are defined by both qualitative and quantitative attributes. Any ministry can *measure* the attributes of its personal relationships in order to evaluate the impacts it is making.

KPI is an acronym for "Key Performance Indicators." KPI's help organizations measure information that is critical to their success. Common KPI's in business include financial ratios, customer service metrics, product failures, and more, which define how efficiently and effectively a business is operating.

Ministries can utilize KPI's as well. Common ministry KPI's include growth of church attendance, quantity of volunteers, quantity of new members, and quantity of people served within various service audience contexts. If your ministry is already doing this, I commend your efforts, but don't stop there. These KPI's are useful for evaluating the "quantity" of relationships within your ministry, however, if only the quantity of relationships is being measured, you are only telling half the story.

While it's great to have a large ministry team, an extensive database of prospective and current financial partners, multiple service audiences, and an abundance of volunteers, in most cases, the quantity of relationships is not as important as the quality. If your ministry has a quantitative KPI of "175 new memberships in 2014," dig deeper to create *qualitative* sub-KPI's. In other words, out of your 175 new members, how many were baptized, how many contributed financially, how many referred others to your ministry, or how many went on a mission trip? Communicating both the quantitative and qualitative attributes of the information you manage will help tell the complete story.

Johnny Evans, Eastern NC Director of FCA, provided the following comments on the importance of relationships to the Triangle FCA ministry:

> *Managing relationships is at the core of everything we do at the Triangle FCA office. Christian ministries should be built upon the foundation of relationships, since that is what Jesus did during His earthly ministry. With our donors, we encourage the building of relationships rather than solely looking to them for a financial transaction. With our coaches, we try to determine their spiritual needs before leveraging their influence throughout the sports community. With our student athletes, we desire to build strong relational bonds*

so that we might earn the right to have input and impact in their lives. It's important to not only build the quantity of relationships, but to also develop quality relationships that reflect our love of Jesus Christ.

Integrity is one of the core values of the FCA ministry, and we are ever vigilant to ensure that all of our relationships are based on how we might consider others over ourselves. There is no higher priority for us than to build strong relationships throughout our ministry footprint, and I would suggest that be the case for all Christian ministries.

Of all of the principles in this book, managing relationships should come most naturally to any Christian minister—after all, relationships are the foundation for every ministry's purpose and existence. Properly managing relationships should be a top priority for every ministry within each of its Five Key Contexts.

Service Audience

Business Logic. The most successful businesses go above and beyond to form trusting relationships with their customers. Successful businesses want their customers to trust that they have their best interests in mind and care more about the relationship than the money that can be generated from sales. It can take a long time to build this type of rapport, and it doesn't happen by accident. Businesses must be intentional about how they create, strengthen, and maintain customer relationships.

The term "Customer Relationship Management" ("CRM") describes how businesses manage customer relationships by classifying them at various levels. Part of the CRM process involves having a list of qualified prospects that the business believes it can convert into paying customers in the future. By implementing the principles discussed in this book, businesses create sales and marketing strategies with the objective of turning prospects into first-time customers, first-time customers into repeat customers, and repeat customers into long-term, loyal clients. The CRM process requires significant thought and strategy, so customer relationship levels must be continually monitored, classified, and defined.

Ministry Logic. Depending on your ministry model, the types of relationships you create with your service audience(s) will vary based on your expectations and desires as well as theirs. You might build relationships with others online through web-based outreach or by living amongst the people you serve locally or abroad. You might sell information products such as books, CDs, and DVDs or minister to others through radio and television, guiding people in their daily walk with God. Whether your ministry serves a single service audience or multiple service audiences, invest time and effort into understanding the types of relationships that can be developed and how to maximize their potential.

Lee Powell, Lead Pastor at Cedar Creek Church, discusses the importance of properly managing relationships throughout his ministry:

We place a high value on personal relationships. Most people desire community, to feel connected. People are tired of doing life on their own and are looking for real, authentic relationships. People were designed to live life in community, and it provides us as a church, more opportunities to disciple and mentor. Cedar Creek is simply trying to emulate what Jesus did with His followers. He walked, talked, ate, slept, and lived with them all while teaching them. Jesus did everyday life with them. When considering the elements of discipleship, we cannot neglect the significance of a relationship.

There are a few that say our church is too big and feel they are just a number. Our response is to get involved with a lifegroup! A lifegroup is a gathering of people, typically 6-12, who meet to do life together. We invite people to personally feel connected to our church community by joining a lifegroup which helps them to grow their faith in a warm, friendly, and supportive setting. Basically, we want people to grow spiritually and connect with others by going through life together. Our lifegroups develop strong interpersonal relationships and provide great opportunities to pray for and serve one another, which not only benefits our church, but our communities as well.

Cedar Creek is about creating opportunities for personal relationships to develop with Jesus and with other people. I believe that the proper management of relationships is the driver that puts all ministry work in motion.

While every organization has their own way of monitoring relationships, below are seven generic relationship levels that your ministry can use (adapted from the business context) to appropriately establish, strengthen, and maintain relationships with those it serves:

Relationship Level	Business Use	Ministry Use
Level 1 – Unaware	The prospective customer is "cold," meaning they know nothing about the business and the business has not contacted or worked with them in the past. The prospect is on the business's target list because it has been qualified as a potential customer based on what the business offers and the market intelligence it has gathered. The business needs to implement an interest generation strategy to gain their attention, establish credibility, and begin building a relationship.	This individual in your service audience is "cold," meaning they do not know anything about your ministry and your ministry has never served them or contacted them in the past. You need to determine how to generate their interest, gain their time and attention, establish credibility, and attempt to build a foundation for a relationship.

Level 2 – Aware	The prospective customer has an awareness of who the business is, but has never made a purchase. The business needs to further educate the prospect in regards to what it offers and how its products and/or services are superior to the competition.	This individual is a member of your service audience and has a basic understanding of your ministry and what it does. Your ministry needs to create opportunities to educate them further about why your ministry exists, what it does, and how it can benefit them.
Level 3 – Informed	The prospective customer understands the business's value proposition, what makes it unique, and how to purchase its product or service. The business should be pursuing regular (and respectful) contact with the prospect without being perceived as too invasive.	This individual is a member of your service audience, understands why your ministry exists, what it does, and how it creates value for others. Your ministry must now determine how to best communicate with them in order to grow the relationship and directly serve them.
Level 4 – Disliking	The prospect has made a single purchase. However, the customer was not satisfied with their purchase or experience for any number of reasons. They are unlikely to make repeat purchases unless the business goes above and beyond to satisfy them. The business must now decide if the customer is worth trying to win back—while many are, some customers aren't worth the time, money, or effort.	Your ministry has directly served this individual and they did not have a positive experience. Your ministry must take action to understand what caused this result. Your ministry must then determine the appropriate steps to (1) serve them again, (2) maintain communication, or (3) provide closure to the relationship in a way that honors the Lord.
Level 5 – Neutral	The prospect has made a single purchase. However, the customer is now showing a lack of interest towards the business. At this level, it is important to get feedback from the customer in order to make an educated decision on whether to invest time, money, and effort in an attempt to recapture their interest.	Your ministry has directly served this individual, and they were not impacted enough to want to engage with your ministry again in the future. You must take action to understand what happened and why. Your ministry must then determine the appropriate steps to (1) serve them again, (2) maintain communication, or (3) provide closure to the relationship in a way that honors the Lord.
Level 6 – Liking	The prospect has made a single purchase. They were satisfied with their purchase and with the business. They have given a positive testimonial and repeat purchases seem likely. Now, the business needs to convert them into a loyal customer.	Your ministry has directly served this individual, and they had a positive experience. Your ministry now needs to determine how to serve them further, in addition to documenting their experience (testimonial) to share with others.
Level 7 – Trusting	The customer has made repeat purchases and is considered a loyal client. They trust the business to consistently satisfy their needs and are delighted to share their positive experiences with others.	Your ministry has served this individual many times. You need to communicate with them regularly, share their experiences, and seek their input on how to develop similar relationships within your service audience.

Developing a cold, prospective relationship into a loyal, trusting one can seem like a daunting task. Business and ministry relationships, however, begin like any other relationship—they start with the fundamentals. Unfortunately, the majority of the population struggles with the following essentials for developing strong relationships: punctuality, communication, integrity, and selflessness. If your ministry can execute these fundamentals with consistency, it will be better positioned to create long-term, trust-worthy relationships.

1. **Punctuality** – 99% of the time, being on time is something you control. If you are consistently late to calls, meetings, and in responding to deadlines, you will be perceived as disrespectful and unprofessional, no matter how smart, accomplished, or capable you are.

2. **Communication** – Most relationship issues occur due to poor communication. A ministry that does not effectively communicate can make others feel uncared for, unsupported, or disrespected. Like punctuality, a ministry's communication methods are completely within its control.

3. **Integrity** – Being a ministry (and person) of integrity means following through on what you say you will do. I'm sad to say that, in my experience, most people (in any context) don't do this consistently. Over-promising and under-delivering is one of the quickest ways to lose credibility and damage a relationship.

4. **Selflessness** – In his book, *How to Win Friends and Influence People*, Dale Carnegie has many practical tips for creating meaningful relationships. One of them is to simply "make the other person feel important—and do it sincerely", in addition to showing a "genuine interest in others."[24] Both tactics can help overcome the barriers that most people face in new relationships.

Financial Partners

Business Logic. When a business attempts to generate interest in new investors, the process is most efficient when relationships are already established. Objectives that might have otherwise taken several months to accomplish may only take days. Once an individual or organization invests into a business, the strength of the relationship will determine the probability of future investments being made.

Ministry Logic. There are three primary ways to establish, strengthen, and maintain trust with your financial partners. First and foremost, document a plan that outlines your goals and strategies so that your financial partners have confidence in giving to your ministry. Whether you are raising money for ongoing ministry operations or for a specific project, having a plan includes:

1. A clear vision and mission.
2. A clear strategy for how the plan will be executed.
3. An overview of why funds are needed and how they will be used.
4. An outline of who will be impacted and when.
5. A projection of the benefits and end results.
6. A method of keeping financial partners up-to-date on critical information and milestones.

The second way to establish, strengthen, and maintain trust with your financial partners is by achieving results. The opportunity to create long-term meaningful relationships will be diminished if you are unable

---

[24] Dale Carnegie, *How To Win Friends and Influence People* (New York City: Simon & Schuster, 1981), 94, 141.

to consistently achieve what you set out to accomplish. However, accomplishing goals exactly as planned, 100% of the time, is not realistic. Ultimately though, financial partners need to feel secure in your ministry's ability to execute the plans it sets forth. As the old saying goes, "The proof is in the pudding."

The third way to establish, strengthen, and maintain trust with your financial partners is to provide them with consistent, meaningful feedback. Financial partners want to see what fruit their investment has produced. Your ministry is the gatekeeper of this information. Think in terms of qualitative and quantitative attributes, and use KPI's to update them on milestones and results. Send email blasts, personal letters, or provide literature summarizing the updates. In addition, post information on your website and use social media to keep them informed. There are numerous ways for your ministry to develop trust with your financial partners through the methods you use to communicate with them.

NOTE – Determine if the seven relationship levels are an effective way of tracking relationships with your financial partners. If so, define each level to make sense for your financial partner context.

Volunteers

Business Logic. Some businesses have a clear distinction between how they treat their customers and how they treat their suppliers. They treat their customers with the utmost care while treating their suppliers as if they are dispensable. The most successful businesses operate with high morals by treating every partner with the same level of respect. Suppliers want to work for companies that appreciate them and value their expertise. Strong supplier relationships can sometimes be the key differentiator between what a business is able to offer in comparison to its competitors. Treating suppliers poorly isn't only the wrong thing to do, it isn't smart.

> *The core of SPS' business was about properly managing relationships. For years, our company worked with a select group of IT integrators and we conducted the majority of our business through them. Within that context, it was critical that we knew who the key people were in regard to generating sales, as well as making sure they liked us and trusted us. As the Director of Sales, I used a version of the seven relationship levels to manage the personal relationships I was developing with each of my customer contacts. This proved to be an invaluable CRM method, especially when the quantity of contacts I worked with exceeded 200.*

> *When it was time to implement projects, properly managing relationships was the key factor in what separated us from our competition. SPS was a team of approximately 80 employees— however, we managed relationships with over 5,000 suppliers located in 100+ countries, through a division in our company called "Relationship Management". This division was dedicated to managing the relationships with our suppliers, which helped us create the strong market reputation we had.*

Ministry Logic. Your ministry may have an abundant supply of first time volunteers. Like anyone doing something for the first time, new volunteers may be nervous. This can happen if they aren't clear about what to expect in their role or if they have doubts about being able to successfully fulfill their responsibilities. While not every volunteer will feel this way, assume that they will by proactively taking action to make them feel calm, confident, and ready to serve. This can include documenting various tasks (what to do and how to do it) as well as being available to answer questions before, during, and after their time of service. This proactive leadership will create trusting relationships because your volunteers will feel valued and appreciated.

If you have volunteers who consistently serve, determine how to best utilize them to promote volunteer opportunities. This can include sharing their testimonials, having them train or lead volunteer groups, or working with them to create or improve volunteer chains. Utilize your veteran volunteers (decide how you define "veteran") as resources to create more value for your volunteer program. Seek out their feedback, consider their input, and provide them with opportunities for their voice to be heard.

NOTE – Determine if the seven relationship levels are an effective way of tracking relationships with your volunteers. If so, define each level for your volunteer context.

Strategic Partners

Business Logic. Strategic partnerships are similar to a marriage, especially when finances, risks, and rewards are shared between the two organizations. Like a marriage, a strategic partnership will only thrive if both organizations trust each other and work hard at the relationship. In most cases, success doesn't just happen. It is an intentional pursuit and the businesses involved must effectively communicate, work towards achieving common goals, and persevere through difficult times together.

Ministry Logic. In ministry, successful strategic partnerships are dependent on a strong mutual trust between both organizations. You may find that it is beneficial for your strategic partnerships to include partial or full disclosure on information related to finances, current and future opportunities, and known or potential threats. Trust will grow as both parties become confident that the other is not withholding pertinent information. Regular communication and face-to-face meetings will also help nurture the relationship to ensure it is built upon a solid foundation.

Staff

Business Logic. For a business to develop strong external relationships, its staff members must be relationship oriented. There is a saying in business that "everyone is a salesperson." This means that every staff member is an ambassador of the business and is responsible for developing new relationships. Businesses must cultivate and emphasize the value of relationships within their own organizations as well. Companies that incrementally host social events or participate in service projects provide their employees with opportunities to build internal relationships—this boosts employee morale, improves organizational culture, and better positions the business for success.

Ministry Logic. No matter what their role, everyone that is a part of a ministry is an ambassador of the organization and an integral part of developing relationships. Similar to business, a ministry's organizational culture is created by its leaders—their personalities, beliefs, values, work ethic, and passions help define who the ministry is. Trustworthy leadership creates trustworthy teams. When trust abounds in an organizational setting, the benefits are evident in how people work, how they serve, and how they pull together during hard times.

Daniel Simmons, The Summit Church's Executive Pastor of Campuses, provided the following comments on the importance of properly managing relationships:

> *Ministry necessitates building and maintaining healthy relationships. Discipleship happens in relationships, and the dynamics of relationships require consistent attention and evaluation. There may be no area more susceptible to the deceitfulness of sin than how we think about and view one another. Distrust, suspicion, and gossip are cancers that undermine the very reason a ministry exists. At Summit, we consistently train our staff on how to properly manage relationships with those internal and external to our organization.*

> *A core value that sets the tone for our internal relationships is that we believe the best about one another and give each other the benefit of the doubt until proven otherwise. This attitude facilitates trust, communication, and accountability. Several times a year, we remind and train our staff on how to do this well. We actively fight the creation of "ministry silos" and strive to work together as a team towards fulfilling our vision and achieving our mission. We have placed the highest value on building healthy and mutually empowering relationships with one another, our partners, and those we serve. This should be a focus for every Christian ministry in order to live out the calling God has for them.*

Relationships are about trust, and most people simply want to know that the other person cares. Theodore Roosevelt said it best, "People don't care how much you know until they know how much you care." You can have all the talent in the world, but if you treat people poorly, you will not amount to much of anything in the end.

Visualize

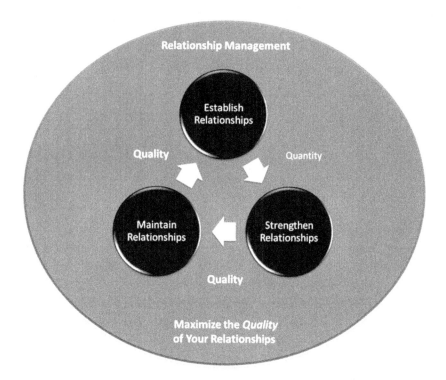

The *Why* Chain

A smart ministry understands the importance of properly managing relationships.

- Why?
    - o Strong relationships are vital to a ministry's success.
- Why?
    - o High quality relationships create trust, which results in the most efficient and effective ministry operations.
- Why?
    - o Trust removes obstacles that may have prevented a ministry from maximizing its potential.

Rhyme *for* Reason

- ❖ *Creating quality relationships*
- ❖ *Is critical for the success,*
- ❖ *Of your ministry's ability*
- ❖ *To always function at its best.*

❖ *Let the growth of your ministry*
❖ *Be based on strong relationships throughout,*
❖ *Because if relationships are shallow,*
❖ *The light you shine may soon be out.*

Scriptural Application

Bible Verse

Matthew 4:19–"'Come, follow me,' Jesus said, 'and I will send you out to fish for people.'"

Commentary

As Christians, we know that Jesus came to save, redeem, and create disciples in order to take His message of love and forgiveness to a hurting and lost world. While Jesus was in human form on Earth, He could have summoned the powers of Heaven to accomplish the mission that was set out before Him. However, He chose to accomplish His work through regular people by establishing, strengthening, and maintaining relationships with a small group of disciples that would later embark on a journey to change the world. Jesus' entire ministry was, and is, directed towards restoring broken relationships between man and God and bringing the Kingdom of God to Earth through His followers. There is no denying the eternal value Jesus places on relationships.

*See pages 202-206 for "Action Questions" related to this principle.

Bringing It All Together

The 12 Principles in this book provide Christian ministries with a strategic operating framework to help maximize their potential to impact people's lives for the Gospel. Let us conclude by summarizing the overall value of each principle with "so that" statements, as we learned about in chapter six.

1. Value the importance of having vision and being able to execute *so that* your ministry is clear on *why* it exists, *what* it is striving to do, and *how* its goals will be achieved.
2. Value the importance of gathering market intelligence *so that* your ministry can use this information to serve others as efficiently and effectively as possible.
3. Value the importance of maximizing your ministry's credibility *so that* it is perceived and experienced as authentic and trustworthy.
4. Value the importance of problem awareness *so that* your ministry understands problems at both the macro and micro levels.
5. Value the importance of understanding problem implications *so that* your ministry can proactively prevent negative consequences from occurring.
6. Value the importance of creating beneficial solutions *so that* risks are reduced and positive outcomes are generated.
7. Value the importance of strategically positioning your ministry *so that* it properly leverages what makes it unique.
8. Value the importance of generating interest in others *so that* your ministry creates as many service and partnering opportunities as possible.
9. Value the importance of creating urgency in others *so that* your ministry can do more in less time.
10. Value the importance of properly handling objections *so that* your ministry can learn from others and speak truth into information that is misunderstood.
11. Value the importance of leveraging testimonials *so that* your ministry can impact others through personal stories.
12. Value the importance of managing relationships *so that* your ministry maximizes the quality of its relationships with others.

The Smart Ministry is a book for the Christian minister. Whether you are part of a church, a Christian non-profit, or enrolled in seminary, my prayer is that this book is a lifelong resource for you. Use *The Smart Ministry* as a practical guide to help you accomplish what God has called you to do. Apply knowledge, in obedience to God, and trust Him with the results.

Part 2 – The *"How"*
The 12 Principles in Action

Take your time when going through the following "Action Questions" and pray through them individually and in a group setting. What may be days or weeks of brainstorming will result in ideas and solutions that can be beneficial for years. Use the space provided to write notes and ideas as you go through each question.

TIP: Read through all of the questions first without answering them. Then, focus on ones that are the most relevant to your position and circumstances at this time. If possible, designate individuals or teams to do the same, in order to maximize the value each question can create across each of your ministry's Five Key Contexts.

Principle #1 in Action: Vision and Execution

Beliefs and Values

- What does your ministry believe about the Bible, about Jesus, and the essential doctrines of what it means to be a Christ follower?

- What does your ministry value (traits or characteristics that you want to be defined by)?

- In what ways can you ensure that your beliefs and values are the cornerstone of your ministry's decisions and actions?

- How can you ensure that those internal and external to your ministry are clear on what your beliefs and values are?

Creating or Refining Your Vision

- Why does your ministry exist?

- What does your ministry want to ultimately achieve (ultimate goal: think in terms of a goal that might exceed your lifetime)?

- What does your ministry want to become?

- Why has God called you to work in this ministry?

- What statement best summarizes the vision of your ministry, and how can you be sure those internal and external to your organization are aware of it?

Creating or Refining Your Mission

- What is your ministry striving to do?

- What do you want your ministry to do or provide?

- What impact does your ministry want to make?

- Who does your ministry want to make a difference for?

- What statement best summarizes the mission of your ministry, and how can you be sure those internal and external to your organization are aware of it?

Strategy and Execution

While the remaining 11 principles are all part of executing your vision and mission, the following questions can help create the framework for your ministry's operations. Please refer to Appendix 1 for additional questions and "Featured Resources" to aid your ministry's operations.

SWOT Analysis

- **Strengths**
    - o What are your ministry's strengths?

    - o How can you better leverage your strengths to execute your vision and mission?

    - o In what ways can your ministry improve on your strengths or create new strengths?

- **Weaknesses**
    - o What are your ministry's weaknesses?

    - o In what ways can you strengthen your areas of weakness?

o   What opportunities can be created by strengthening these areas of weakness?

- **Opportunities**
    o   What opportunities do you have to better serve those within your Five Key Contexts?

    o   What opportunities exist to create new service audiences in order to serve more people?

    o   What unique serving or partnering opportunities may only be present for a select window of time? How can you capitalize on these opportunities?

- **Threats**
    o   What known threats face your ministry today?

    o   In what ways can you better manage, neutralize, or eliminate known threats?

    o   In what ways can you prepare for future or potential threats?

- How does your ministry plan to fulfill its vision?

- How does your ministry plan to achieve its mission?

Staff Context – Questions to Assist with Strategic Planning and Execution

- Ministry Operations
  - o What kinds of _____ do you need to begin or operate your ministry?
    - Talent:

    - Experience:

    - Personalities:

    - Expertise:

  - o What are the different methods or avenues for identifying the people you need?

  - o Once you find the people you need, how can you attract them to your ministry?

- Organizational Structure
    - o What *essential* staff positions need to be filled, and what is the optimal organizational structure (org chart) for your ministry to operate with the highest levels of effectiveness (quality) and efficiency (speed) within your allotted budgets (cost)?

- Job Expectations
    - o What results are expected for each job function within your ministry?

- o Does each staff member have a clear understanding of what is expected of them? If not, in what ways can you make job expectations clearer?

- o In what ways can you provide better training for your staff members on what is expected of them in their role in addition to how to achieve expected outcomes?

- Longevity
  - o Does your ministry have a high rate of staff turnover? If so, what causes it, and how can you improve so that you are able to retain employees for longer periods of time?

  - o In what ways can you create greater incentive for your staff to want to stay with your ministry for the long haul?

- Bible Knowledge
  - o Is there a base level of Bible knowledge or key Scripture memory that you desire your staff members to have?

    - If so, in what ways can you ensure this knowledge is known, understood, and lived out every day?

o   What opportunities can your ministry create to increase Bible knowledge among your staff and volunteers?

- Autonomous Leadership
    o   Is autonomous leadership encouraged within your ministry?

    o   In what ways can you promote leadership and autonomy within your ministry at all levels?

    o   In what ways can you help your staff members to lead themselves more effectively?

    o   In what ways can you remove your staff's fear of decision making and of making mistakes in order for them to consistently operate with high-levels of confidence?

- Financial Management
    o   What can you do to help your ministry's staff better manage budgets for various cost categories of your ministry?

    o   What processes can your ministry develop to ensure that the products and services it needs are being purchased in the most cost effective way without compromising the desired value/quality?

- How can you ensure your staff members understand the importance of tithing and proper financial stewardship?

- In what ways can you leverage the financial expertise of people outside of your ministry to benefit your staff members?

- Project Management
  - How efficient is your ministry at planning and managing projects or events?

  - In what areas is your ministry unorganized and how can you improve in these areas?

  - In what ways can your ministry better manage and plan projects or events?

- Marketing
  - Does your ministry have staff members that are proficient in the areas of branding, marketing, or creative design? How can you better leverage their talents?

  - In what ways can you better leverage the branding and marketing talents of those external to your ministry?

- Technical
    - o Does your ministry have staff members that are proficient in the areas of electronic equipment, sound systems, IT (information technology), or audio/visual systems? How can you better leverage their talents?

    - o In what ways can you better leverage the technical talents of those external to your ministry?

- Task Management
    - o What tasks occur regularly within your ministry that should have a documented process in order to create "standard operating procedures"?

TIP: Any task that happens more than once should have a documented process

    - o In what ways can you utilize documented processes to train current and new staff members on how to correctly implement various tasks?

Principle #2 in Action: Market Intelligence

Market Analysis

- How does your ministry define its "total service audience" (everyone within a service audience that your ministry aims to serve)?

- In what ways can you segment the total service audience to create one or more target service audiences?

- What are your goals per target service audience, and are there time periods that you want to achieve each goal by?

- Does each goal support your ministry's overall vision and mission? If not, how can you adjust them so that they support your vision and mission?

- What "barriers to entry" need to be avoided or overcome in order to begin serving your target service audience(s)?

Service Audience

- What promise can your ministry make them (target service audience) that reflects the unique value it is able to offer?

    o In what ways can you ensure that your ministry understands how to consistently deliver upon this promise?

    o What would be the result of *not* delivering upon this promise?

- Perceptions/Beliefs
    o What are their perceptions about Christianity?

- What false perceptions exist and why do you think they exist?

- What can you do to clear up any false perceptions?

o What do they believe about Jesus?

o What do they believe their purpose in life is?

o How should their beliefs and perceptions affect how you minister to them?

- Expectations
    o What do they expect from _____ and are these expectations accurate? How can you help them reset their expectations based on truth from Scripture?
        - God:

        - Themselves:

        - Their Family:

        - Your Ministry:

- Interpretations of Value
  - o What do they value (what is important to them)?

  - o Do they see the value in a personal relationship with Jesus? If not, why, and what can your ministry do to show them this immeasurable value?

  - o What value do they place on themselves, family, or others?

  - o How can your ministry serve them better through understanding what they value?

- Motivations
  - o What motivates them to want to do good?

  - o How can you motivate them to be concerned about what matters to God?

  - o In what ways can your ministry tap into their motivations to serve them better?

Understanding your target service audience's perceptions, beliefs, expectations, interpretations of value, and motivations can have many positive impacts on the other key contexts of your ministry. Applying the principle of market intelligence, however, is not exclusive to your target service audience(s). Your ministry's financial partners, volunteers, strategic partners, and staff members have their own perceptions, beliefs, expectations, interpretations of value, and motivations as well. If understood, your ministry will be able to use this intelligence to develop the most trusting, relevant, and beneficial relationships possible.

Financial Partners

- What promise can your ministry make them (financial partners) that reflects the unique value it is able to offer?

    o What would be the result of *not* delivering upon this promise?

- Expectations
    o What do they expect to know ***before*** investing in your ministry?

        ▪ Where is your ministry currently lacking on meeting these expectations?

        ▪ In what ways can you meet or exceed their expectations?

    o What do they expect to receive ***after*** investing in your ministry?

- Where is your ministry currently lacking on meeting these expectations?

- In what ways can you meet or exceed their expectations?

- Interpretations of Value
  - What do they deem as "valuable ROIs" (return on investments) after investing in your ministry?

    - In what ways can you ensure that they stay informed of the results their contributions are helping to achieve (high-level reporting as well as detailed reporting)?

- Motivations
  - What factors motivate them to want to invest in your ministry?

    - In what ways can your ministry tap into those motivations to maximize your chances of securing financial investments?

Volunteers

- What promise can your ministry make them (volunteers) that reflects the unique value it is able to offer?

    o   What would be the result of *not* delivering upon this promise?

- Expectations
  - o   What do they expect to know or receive ***before*** volunteering?

    - Where is your ministry currently lacking on meeting these expectations?

    - In what ways can you meet or exceed their expectations?

- Interpretations of Value
  - o   What do they value in regard to volunteering (what's important to them)?

    - How can you create volunteer experiences that they deem as valuable?

- Motivations
  - o   What factors motivate them to want to volunteer?

o In what ways can your ministry tap into those motivations to maximize volunteer commitments?

Strategic Partners

- What promise can your ministry make them (strategic partners) that reflects the unique value it is able to offer?

  o What would be the result of *not* delivering upon this promise?

- Expectations
  o What do they expect to know ***before*** partnering with your ministry?

    - Where is your ministry currently lacking on meeting these expectations?

    - In what ways can you meet or exceed their expectations?

  o What do they expect to receive ***after*** partnering with your ministry?

- Where is your ministry currently lacking on meeting these expectations?

- In what ways can you meet or exceed their expectations?

- Interpretations of Value
  - What value do they want to experience or create in the strategic partnership?

- Motivations
  - What factors might motivate them to want to partner with your ministry?

  - In what ways can your ministry tap into those motivations?

Staff

- What promise can your ministry make them (staff members) that reflects the unique value it is able to offer?

  - What would be the result of *not* delivering upon this promise?

- Expectations
  - What do they expect to know ***before*** joining your ministry?

      - Where is your ministry currently lacking on meeting these expectations?

      - In what ways can you meet or exceed their expectations?

  - What do they expect ***after*** joining your ministry?

      - Where is your ministry currently lacking on meeting these expectations?

      - In what ways can you meet or exceed their expectations?

- Interpretations of Value
  - What value do they want to experience or create by working with your ministry?

- Motivations
    - o What factors motivate them to want to work with your ministry?

    - o In what ways can you tap into those motivations to retain valuable staff?

Principle #3 in Action: Maximizing Credibility

If you understand what it means to have personal credibility and want to be viewed as a credible person, it is within your control to make it happen. Furthermore, if you know your ministry is lacking in certain areas that are negatively impacting its credibility, it has the ability to make the necessary adjustments to improve.

Use the "Personal Credibility" questions below in two ways. First, ask yourself and be honest about your current strengths and weaknesses. Second, ask someone else these questions as they relate to you personally. You will benefit from the feedback provided by an outside perspective.

Personal Credibility:

- Do you view yourself as a credible, trustworthy person? Why or why not?

  o Do others view you as a credible, trustworthy person? Why or why not?

  o In what ways can you work to become more credible and trustworthy?

- Are you on time or are you often late?

  o What can you do to ensure that you are on time to commitments you've made and that you respond in a timely manner to other's communication?

- Do you have the necessary knowledge to effectively execute your job functions?

    o   In what ways can you further increase your knowledge and competencies in order to perform at consistent, high-levels of quality?

- Do you interrupt people during conversations because you are eager to get your point across?

    o   In what ways can you improve your patience and sincerity as a listener?

- Are you viewed by others as reliable?

    o   In what ways can you consistently become more reliable?

- Do you put 100% effort into your job? Random tasks? Service projects?

    o   In what ways can you work harder and smarter in all you do?

o   Do you look at each task set before you as an opportunity to honor God and worship Him?

- Are you overly critical or judgmental?

    o   What areas require you to love yourself better (or give yourself a break) in order to prevent passing negative emotions on to others?

    o   In what ways can you balance constructive criticism with positive reinforcement?

- Do you gossip about others behind their back?

    o   How can you work harder to see the good in those that are difficult to work with and show grace towards the people you perceive as negative?

- Do you treat people different based on what they can do for you?

    o   How can you ensure that you are kind and authentic to everyone you encounter, regardless of their success, position, or title?

- Do you consistently tell others what to do without seeking their input?

    o In what ways can you foster greater teamwork with those you work with?

Organizational Credibility:

- Aside from the principles within this book, what other factors contribute to your ministry's credibility and its ability to build trust within each of its Five Key Contexts?
    o Service audiences?

    o Financial partners?

Reminder: At a minimum, ensure your financial partners are always aware of the following:

- ✓ The use of funds (why they are needed and what they are needed for).
- ✓ Who will be impacted (service audience or others).
- ✓ When the impacts will be made.
- ✓ The expected results that will be achieved.
- ✓ The actual results that are achieved.

o   Volunteers?

o   Strategic partners?

o   Staff members?

Principle #4, #5, and #6 in Action: Problem Awareness, Problem Implications, and Solution Benefits

- ✓ **Problem Awareness**: Understanding problems at the 200-mile-view as well as what causes them.
- ✓ **Problem Implications:** Understanding what will or might happen if problems are not resolved.
- ✓ **Solution Benefits:** Positive outcomes and/or avoided consequences.

Service Audience

- What physical and spiritual problems does or can your ministry solve for your service audience, and what is the root cause of each problem?

  - o In what ways can you better understand the cause and dynamics of each problem?

o What will or might occur if each problem isn't solved?

o Who will or might be impacted if each problem isn't solved?

o When will or might the impact occur if each problem isn't solved?

- Do your ministry's solutions produce positive outcomes and/or benefits that reduce/eliminate risk?

o   If so, what feedback from your service audience do you have validating this?

o   If so, are there ways to provide additional positive outcomes? What are they?

o   If so, are there ways for your service audience to avoid or eliminate other risks as well? What are they?

- Do your solution benefits produce the desired/needed results? Do they give others hope?

Financial Partners

- How do you currently educate financial partners on your ministry's financial needs?

- In what ways can you increase their understanding of your financial needs—for ministry operations in addition to outreach efforts?

- What will or might happen if the needed funds for operations and outreach efforts are not raised?

  o How can you ensure your financial partners are aware of these implications?

o How can you use these implications to motivate your financial partners to give to your ministry?

- What positive outcomes will your financial partners' contributions provide to your ministry's operations and outreach efforts?

- What risks or negative consequences will your financial partners' contributions help your ministry avoid (operations and outreach efforts)?

- How can you ensure that your financial partners understand the benefits and results their contributions will help provide?

Volunteers

- Is your ministry successful at determining the types and quantity of volunteers needed for a specific event or on-going purposes? If not, what can you do to better determine the types and quantities of volunteers your ministry needs?

- What problems do volunteers solve for your ministry?

  o Create a "volunteer-chain" outlining key volunteer tasks (problems they solve for your ministry) and how they impact other people or areas of your ministry:

- What will or might happen if your volunteer chain malfunctions at one or multiple levels?

o How can you prevent these malfunctions from occurring?

o What back-up plans can you implement in the event there is an issue in your volunteer chain?

o How can you ensure volunteers understand the benefits they create for your ministry (positive outcomes and avoided risks)?

Strategic Partners

- What problems are you aware of that a strategic partnership might appropriately address?

- What will or might happen if your ministry doesn't create the necessary strategic partnerships?

- In what ways can you ensure that your strategic partners clearly understand why joining with your ministry will address existing problems (your problems, theirs, and others)?

- What positive outcomes will the strategic partnership create?

- What risks or consequences will the strategic partnership help avoid?

Staff

- What problems exist that can only be resolved by your ministry's staff members?

- What are the implications if these problems aren't appropriately resolved?

    o How can you ensure that your staff members are adequately equipped to address these problems?

Problem Awareness and Problem Implications Tip: Create a "lessons learned" document in Excel, Word, or other program. The purpose of the document will be to record problems your ministry has faced, mistakes it has made, etc. Record the date of the learning experience and what has now been implemented to prevent the issue from recurring. This will ensure that everyone is knowledgeable of past problems/ risks/mistakes, as well as how to avoid similar negative outcomes in the future.

Principle #7 in Action: Strategic Positioning

Answer the following questions as they relate to your ministry as a whole:

- What makes your ministry different from other ministries?

- How does your ministry's differentiation enable it to create unique value for others?

- How does your ministry's differentiation enable it to uniquely impact people's lives for the Gospel?

- How do you want your ministry to be perceived and why do you want it to be perceived this way?

- In what ways can you ensure that your ministry is perceived this way?

- In what ways can you ensure that your ministry tangibly backs up the perceptions it creates?

Service Audience

- In what ways do you currently serve others that are unique compared to other ministries?

- What can your ministry do to strengthen the unique value it provides to your service audiences?

Financial Partners

- What are the unique elements of your ministry that attract financial partners to want to invest?

- How can you use the AUR Method to help increase the probabilities of obtaining financial investments?

TIP: Present the following information to your financial partners:

A (Audience)

- ✓ Key information from your "market analysis" (refer to chapter 2).
- ✓ Description of *how* the target service audience is already being served.
- ✓ Validation that your ministry's solutions can provide the target service audience what it needs.

U (Uniqueness)

- ✓ Your ministry's attributes that enable it serve the target service audience better or differently than conventional methods (intellectual property, experience, expertise, partnerships, etc.).
- ✓ A description of how your ministry will achieve its goals.

R (Results)

- ✓ Since financial partners won't be receiving financial returns (like business investors), outline the results their contributions will help achieve through providing metrics (quantitative and qualitative) that measure the success of your ministry's outreach efforts.

- What investments can you make in your ministry model (tangible or intangible) in order to attract financial partners to want to invest?

Volunteers

- How important are volunteers (volunteer chain) in the creation and delivery of your ministry's value to your service audience(s)?

- In what ways can you increase the value your ministry offers through utilizing volunteers?

Strategic Partners

- How can your ministry leverage strategic partnerships to create increased value for those within your other key contexts?

Staff

- Do your ministry's staff members clearly understand your ministry model, how it creates/delivers value, and what makes it unique?

- In what ways can your ministry's staff members strengthen your value proposition as it is experienced by others in each of your key contexts?

General

- What do you want people to associate with your ministry?

- What symbols, images, or colors best represent the identity and personality of your ministry?

Principle #8 in Action: Interest Generation

Interest Generation Tips:

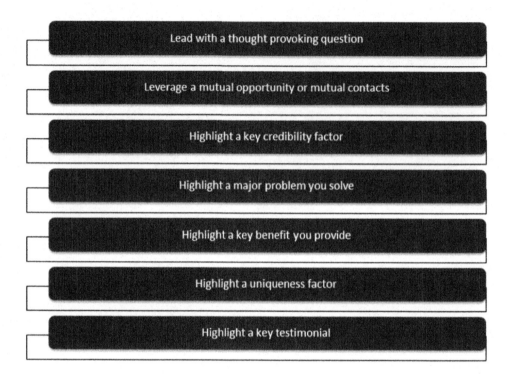

- Lead with a thought provoking question
- Leverage a mutual opportunity or mutual contacts
- Highlight a key credibility factor
- Highlight a major problem you solve
- Highlight a key benefit you provide
- Highlight a uniqueness factor
- Highlight a key testimonial

Service Audience

- In what ways can you generate interest within your target service audience(s) so that they want to learn more about your ministry: why it exists, what it does, and how it does it?

- How can you customize the seven generic interest generation strategies to create additional service and outreach opportunities?

TIP: Co-create interest generation strategies with your target service audience(s) to minimize assumptions about what interests them.

Financial Partners

- In what ways can you generate interest in the minds of current and prospective financial partners so that they want to contribute or continue contributing to your ministry?

- How can you customize the seven generic interest generation strategies to create additional partnering opportunities with your financial partners?

TIP: Co-create interest generation strategies with your financial partners to minimize assumptions about what interests them.

Volunteers

- In what ways can you generate interest in the minds of current or prospective volunteers so that they want to learn more about the volunteer opportunities available within your ministry?

- How can you customize the seven generic interest generation strategies to attract the types and quantity of volunteers you need?

TIP: Co-create interest generation strategies with your volunteers to minimize assumptions about what interests them.

Strategic Partners

- In what ways can you generate interest in the minds of prospective strategic partners so that they want to learn more about partnership opportunities?

- How can you customize the seven generic interest generation strategies to attract the types of partners you desire to work with?

Staff

- How can you customize the seven interest generation strategies to attract and retain the staff your ministry needs?

- How can your staff use the seven interest generation strategies to create additional service and partnership opportunities through the following channels?

    o **Personal interaction**: one-on-one or group settings.

    o **Programs or events:** catered towards specific purposes.

    o **Website**: look & feel, messaging, updates, blog, storytelling, pictures, milestones, statistics.

    o **Social Media**: updates, collaborations, partnerships, information sharing.

- o **Radio & TV**: radio shows, sermons, selling information products (books, CD's, study guides, etc.).

- o **Email**: email marketing.

- o **Literature**: brochures / pamphlets, booklets, CD's, downloads.

- What follow up processes do you have (and need) in place when someone is interested in your ministry and wants to learn more?

- How can you ensure that someone who is interested in your ministry receives a prompt response?

Principle #9 in Action: Creating Urgency

Urgency Creation Tips:

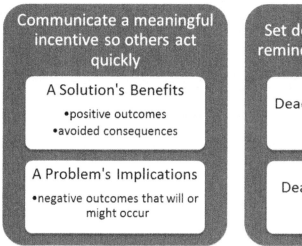
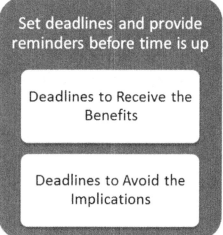

Service Audience

- How urgent is your ministry in meeting the needs of your service audience(s)? In what areas can you increase your ministry's urgency in responding to their needs?

- How can you customize and utilize the urgency creation tips to motivate your service audience(s) to solve their problems?

- How can you customize and utilize the generic urgency creation tips to create additional opportunities to serve?

Financial Partners

- In what ways can you customize and utilize the urgency creation tips to increase the probability of raising needed funds?

Volunteers

- In what ways can you customize and utilize the urgency creation tips to increase the probability of obtaining the types and quantity of volunteers your ministry needs?

Strategic Partners

- In what ways can you customize and utilize the urgency creation tips to increase the probability of obtaining the types and quantity of strategic partners your ministry needs?

Staff

- In what ways can you customize and utilize the urgency creation tips to increase the amount of urgency your staff members operate with on a daily basis?

- What would incent *you* to operate at higher levels of urgency within your role?

Principle #10 in Action: Handling Objections

✓ <u>**Process for handling valid objections:**</u>

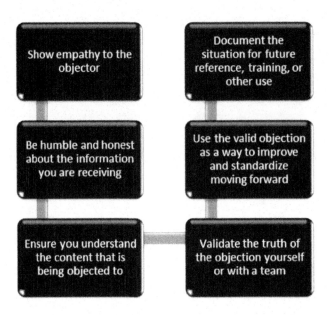

- How can you ensure your ministry is improving in response to the *valid* objections it receives from those within your:
    - o   Service Audience context?

    - o   Financial Partner context?

     o   Volunteer context?

     o   Strategic Partner context?

     o   Staff context?

✓   **Process for handling Invalid Objections:**

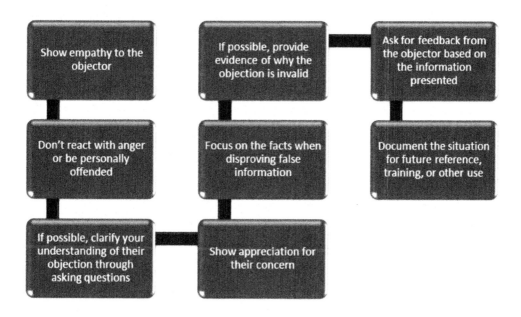

- How can you ensure your ministry is properly responding to the *invalid* objections it receives from those within your:
    o   Service Audience context?

    o   Financial Partner context?

    o   Volunteer context?

    o   Strategic Partner context?

    o   Staff context?

Principle #11 in Action: Leveraging Testimonials

✓ **All-Out-Positive Testimonial:** A testimonial that focuses on all the positive aspects of one's experience.
✓ **Reverse Testimonial:** A testimonial that begins with one or more objections, but concludes with how the objections were proved to be invalid.

Service Audience

- How does your ministry currently capture the experiences of those it has served in the past?

- How can you leverage testimonials (all-out-positive and reverse testimonials) within each of your key contexts to help your ministry impact its service audience(s)?

Financial Partners

- How can your ministry leverage testimonials (all-out-positive and reverse testimonials) within each of its key contexts to help current or future financial partners see the value in contributing to your ministry?

- What opportunities exist to leverage testimonials from third-party authorities or experts that will help give your financial partners confidence in investing?

- How can you leverage the success of other ministries to give your financial partners confidence in investing in your vision, mission, strategy, or ministry model?

Volunteers

- How can you leverage the testimonials (all-out-positive and reverse testimonials) within each of your key contexts to motivate new volunteers to sacrifice their time for your ministry?

Strategic Partners

- In what ways can your ministry leverage the testimonials (all-out-positive and reverse testimonials) within each of your key contexts to help future strategic partners see the value in partnering with your ministry?

Staff

- In what ways can you leverage testimonials (all-out-positive and reverse testimonials) within each of your key contexts to attract new hires to your ministry?

All Contexts

- How can your ministry use the following platforms to share testimonials with others?
  - o Website:

  - o Video:

  - o Brochures:

  - o Case Studies:

  - o Social Media:

  - o Email:

  - o Radio:

  - o Television:

  - o Books:

  - o Other:

Principle #12 in Action: Managing Relationships

All Key Contexts

- What types of relationships does your ministry desire and expect to create with your:
  - Service Audience(s)?

  - Financial Partners?

  - Volunteers?

  - Strategic Partners?

  - Staff?

- What types of relationships do your _____ desire and expect from your ministry, and how can you be sure to meet or exceed their expectations?
  - Service Audience(s):

o   Financial Partners:

o   Volunteers:

o   Strategic Partners:

o   Staff:

- How does your ministry currently track relationship levels with those within your
    _____ context?
    o   Service Audience(s):

    o   Financial Partners:

    o   Volunteers:

    o   Strategic Partners:

o   Staff:

Reminder: Consider redefining the relationship levels for each key context as outlined in chapter 12.

- What are the "key success factors" to maximize the quality of relationships with your:
  o   Service Audience(s)?

  o   Financial Partners?

  o   Volunteers?

o   Strategic Partners?

o   Staff?

- What quantitative and qualitative KPIs (Key Performance Indicators) can be created to summarize the relationships you have within your Five Key Contexts?

Key Context	Quantitative KPI	Qualitative KPI
Service Audience(s)		
Financial Partners		
Volunteers		
Strategic Partners		
Staff		

APPENDIX 1
The 12 Principles and the Gospel

The Smart Ministry demonstrates how the 12 Principles can help any ministry operate at its highest potential, while still remaining under the authority of God. Beyond the organizational setting, each principle has broader applications as well. They can be of value in everyday life, but more importantly, they can be valuable in helping to frame and communicate the Gospel message.

The following questions display how the 12 Principles can be used in sequential order when presenting the Gospel in a one-on-one or group setting. As with every other "Action Question," give these questions adequate thought and prayer in order to create the best ideas possible to support your efforts. Brainstorm on the questions in groups and pray that God will use them to help frame the Gospel message with as much relevancy and clarity as possible. As Martin Luther once said, "Unless the Gospel is preached with contemporary relevance, it has not been preached."

Vision and Execution

- Does your ministry operate upon beliefs and values that reflect the Gospel?

- Is your ministry's vision Gospel centered?

- Is your ministry's mission Gospel centered?

- In what ways can your ministry display the Gospel in how it executes its vision and mission?

- What Scripture can you reference to explain God's vision and plan for mankind?

- What Scripture can you reference to show how God is executing His plans through Jesus, the Holy Spirit, and the Church?

Market Intelligence

- How can you utilize this principle to preach the Gospel with relevance to your audience (one-on-one or in a large setting)?

Interest Generation

- What Scripture can you reference to generate interest in others to want to learn more about the Bible and about God?

- What biblical facts or statistics can you reference to generate interest in others to want to learn more about Jesus?

- How can you utilize the seven generic interest generation strategies to create opportunities to share the Gospel?

Strategic Positioning

- What Scripture can you reference to show who God is and who God isn't to ensure that His true identity is accurately portrayed?

- What Scripture can you reference to explain why Jesus is the most unique person that has ever lived and why Christianity is unique compared to all other "religions"?

- In what ways can you ensure that the Bible is being communicated for what it is: The Word of God?

Maximizing Credibility

- What Scripture can you reference to authenticate the credibility (trustworthiness) of the Bible and of Jesus when sharing the Gospel?

- What other historical evidence can you reference to authenticate the credibility (trustworthiness) of the Bible and of Jesus when sharing the Gospel?

- How can you personally show credibility when sharing the Gospel to create trust with those you are speaking to/with?

Problem Awareness

- How can you use this principle to ensure that your audience is aware of the sin problem we are all born with?

- What Scripture can you reference to bring awareness to everyone's sin problem?

- How can you personally testify about the awareness of your sin and the awareness of your need for Jesus?

- What Scripture can you reference to create awareness about who the devil is, how sin came into our lives, and how helpless we are without Jesus?

Problem Implications

- What are the temporal and eternal implications of not being in a personal relationship with Jesus? What Scripture can you reference to support these implications?

- How can you personally testify about the implications of your sin and how these implications have created a deep desire for you to know Jesus?

Solution Benefits

- What Scripture can you reference to support how Jesus is the solution to everyone's sin problem?

- What Scripture can you reference to show the benefits of being in a personal relationship with Jesus (positive outcomes and avoided consequences)?

- What benefits have you personally experienced through placing your faith in Jesus?

Handling Objections

- Generally speaking, what are common invalid objections that most non-believers have about the Gospel?

  o Would it be helpful to proactively address these objections and use Scripture to support why they are invalid?

- If different than above, what are the common invalid objections the people *within your target service audience(s)* have about the Gospel?

  o Would it be helpful to proactively address these objections and use Scripture to support why they are invalid?

- What objections aren't clearly answered in the Bible and how can you address them so that God is glorified in your response?

Leveraging Testimonials

- What testimonials from Scripture can you reference to support the truth about Jesus?

- What personal testimony can you reference to describe what Jesus has done in your life?

- What third-party testimonials can you reference to show how Jesus has impacted the lives of others?

Creating Urgency

- What Scripture can you reference to help communicate the urgency of the Gospel message?

- How can you practically illustrate how fragile life is to help create urgency in others to commit their lives to Jesus?

- How can you re-emphasize the benefits of following Jesus and the implications of not following Him in order to create urgency in others to accept Jesus as their Savior?

Managing Relationships

- How can you intentionally develop relationships with those you share the Gospel with, without being overbearing?

- How can you continue to serve and love the person that is adamantly rejecting the Gospel message or delaying their decision to accept Jesus as their Savior?

- What can you do to help disciple new believers so that they grow in their faith?

APPENDIX 2
Featured Resources

Systems and Technology

Databases
- Information Management
    - o How can you utilize online database systems to manage critical information related to those within each of your Five Key Contexts?

Look into:

Featured Resource	Website	About
Capterra	www.capterra.com	**With over 50** Database Software Systems for ministries, Capterra provides an analyst to help your ministry identify the best software management system specific to your needs.

Website

- Ministry Identity
    - o How effective is your website in communicating the identity of your ministry?

    - o How can you improve your website to more effectively communicate your beliefs, values, vision, mission, and strategy?

o How can you ensure that your website represents how you want others to feel about your ministry?

- Spreading Awareness
  o How can you strategically use your website to reach more people for the Gospel?

- Outsourcing
  o Can you leverage third-party web developers to minimize development costs?

Look into:

Featured Resource	Website
Christian Internet	www.christian-internet.com
Faith Connector	www.faithconnector.com
Faith Highway	www.faithhighway.com
Ministry Designs	www.ministrywebsitedesigns.com
My Church Website	www.mychurchwebsite.com
Share Faith	www.sharefaith.com

Other Website Builders:

Featured Resource	Website
Top 10 Best Website Builders	www.top10bestwebsitebuilders.com

Servers

- Cloud-based Data Storage
  - Does your ministry currently utilize IT hardware, such as servers, to electronically store and manage key documents and information relevant to your ministry?

    - If not, would your ministry benefit from a "cloud-based" server to store, track, and manage key documents, sermons, lessons, videos, processes, etc.?

Look into:

Featured Resource	Website
Box	www.box.com
Drop Box	www.dropbox.com
Google Drive	www.drive.google.com
iCloud	www.icloud.com
JustCloud	www.justcloud.com
OneDrive	www.onedrive.live.com
ShareFile	www.sharefile.com
Smart Box	www.panterranetworks.com
SugarSync	www.sugarsync.com

Audio/Visual Equipment

- Equipment Use
  - o What audio or projector equipment can you utilize to create the desired atmospheres?

Look into:

Featured Resource	Website
Church Audio Supply	www.churchaudiosupply.com
Church Sound Store	www.churchsoundstore.com
Church Technologies	www.church-technologies.com
EZ Pro Gear	www.ezprogear.com
Kingdom Inc.	www.kingdom.com
Pro Acoustics USA	www.proacousticsusa.com

Email Marketing Services

- Standardization of Emails
  - o Do your staff members have matching email addresses? If not, would matching emails create a better perception of credibility and/or unity?

- Email Marketing
  - o How can you utilize email marketing services to spread awareness and news about your ministry to those within each of your Five Key Contexts?

Look into:

Featured Resource	Website
ARC Churches	www.arcchurches.com
Church Buzz	www.churchbuzz.org
Constant Contact	www.constantcontact.com
My Newsletter Builder	www.mynewsletterbuilder.com
Truth Advertising	www.truthadvertising.org

Animated Video Production

- How can you use animated explainer videos to help with fundraising and communicating your vision, mission, strategy, and/or ministry model in a way that is interesting and unique?

Look into:

Featured Resource	Website
Rip Media Group	www.ripmediagroup.com
Switch Video	www.switchvideo.com
*Vision House	www.visionhouse.com

*Created the video featured on *The Smart Ministry* website

Video Conferencing

- Do you currently utilize any video conference or screen sharing applications?

- In what areas can you reduce travel costs by utilizing video conferencing services?

Look into:

Featured Resource	Website
Adobe Connect Pro	www.adobe.com
BlueJeans	www.bluejeans.com
Citrix – GoTo Meeting	www.gotomeeting.com
Fuze	www.fuze.com
Skype	www.skype.com
WebEx	www.webex.com

Contemporary Phone Systems

- Low Cost
  - o Have you looked into free or low-cost phone system options to enable your staff to communicate more effectively?

- Operational Efficiency
  - o Do your office phone systems have call forwarding to mobile device capability?

  - o Would your ministry benefit from a cloud-based phone system?

Look into:

Featured Resource	Website
CallRingTalk	www.callringtalk.com
eVoice	www.evoice.com
Freedom Voice	www.freedomvoice.com
Grasshopper	www.grasshopper.com
Phone Tree	www.phonetree.com
RingCentral	www.ringcentral.com
Sonetel	www.sonetel.com
Talkroute	www.talkroute.com

Social Media

- How can you better utilize social media platforms to **communicate and share** what your ministry is doing?

- How can you utilize social media platforms to **connect** with other people or organizations?

- How can you utilize social media platforms to **learn** about what other ministries are doing?

Look into:

Featured Resource	Website
Buffer	www.buffer.com
Doodle	www.doodle.com
Facebook	www.facebook.com
Four Square	www.foursquare.com
Google+	www.plus.google.com
Group Me	www.groupme.com
LinkedIn	www.linkedin.com
Pinterest	www.pinterest.com
Scoop It	www.scoop.it
The City	www.onthecity.org
Tumblr	www.tumblr.com
Twitter	www.twitter.com
Vimeo	www.vimeo.com
YouTube	www.youtube.com

Financial Management

- Cash Flow
  - How do you currently organize and track all of the costs associated with your ministry?

  - How do you currently manage income for your ministry?

- Outsourced Accounting
    - o Would it be valuable to outsource your accounting needs to a third-party accredited firm?

Look into:

Featured Resource	Website
Capin Crouse LLP	www.capincrouse.com
Dennison & Co.	www.churchcpa.net
Thomas, Judy & Tucker	www.tjtpa.com
Wisdom over Wealth	www.wisdomoverwealth.com

- Cloud Based Financial Management
    - o Would a web-based financial management system benefit your ministry?

Look into:

Featured Resource	Website
Church Pro	www.churchpro.com
ICON Systems	www.iconcmo.com
Shelby Systems	www.shelbysystems.com
Simplify Church	www.simplifychurch.com
Top Small Business Financial Management Systems	www.freshbooks.com www.mint.com www.concur.com www.quickbooks.com

Facilities

- Current Impact
  - How do your facilities make your staff and others feel?

- Desired Impact
  - How do you *want* your facilities to make your staff and others feel?

- The 5 Human Senses
  - How can you utilize sight, smell, sound, taste, and touch to enhance the experience of those that visit your facilities?

- Feasibility
  - What are practical ways to update or modify your facilities to create the experience you want others to have?

Look into:

Featured Resource	Website
BGW Services	www.bgwservices.com
Church Interiors	www.churchinteriors.com
Church Stage Design Ideas	www.churchstagedesignideas.com
JH Batten, Inc.	www.jhbatten.com
NACDB	www.nacdb.com
Sprung	www.sprung.com
*Storr Office Environments	www.storr.com

*The Smart Ministry "Featured Organization"

APPENDIX 3
Lessons Learned

Take a moment to reflect upon 15 lessons I've learned in business and pray about how they might be applicable to your life and your ministry.

Lesson #1: The importance of punctuality

No matter how smart, likeable, or capable you are, you will damage your credibility if you aren't on time. If you are punctual, it shows that you respect others' time. If you are late, it creates a perception of self-centeredness and lack of respect for others. 99% of the time, being punctual is within your control. If you are going to be late, give the other party notice with a brief explanation. Believe me, they will appreciate it. Be cautious though—if you are always late with an explanation, it will become the same as being late without an explanation. Your reputation depends on it—just be on time.

Lesson #2: The importance of organization

In managing any project, more than half the battle is staying organized. You must be able to organize your contacts along with their roles and responsibilities, keep track of finances, manage key documents, and communicate with others via phone, email, text, in person meetings, and more. Having the right systems and processes in place to help stay organized will enable you to:

1. Not feel overwhelmed when managing multiple tasks.
2. Operate efficiently and effectively when workloads increase.
3. Accurately manage expectations concerning commitments you are able to make.

Lesson #3: The importance of managing expectations

Whether it is overseeing a project or operating a ministry, everything comes down to managing expectations. Disappointment usually occurs when results are not what someone expected they would be. The key to managing expectations is honesty and an acute knowledge of the task at hand. If you can properly manage expectations, you will be able to:

1. Clearly represent what your organization does and does not do.
2. Effectively communicate what results can be expected and when.
3. Explain what is required in order to achieve the expected results.
4. Create and implement back-up plans when needed.
5. Prevent over-promising and under-delivering.

Lesson #4: The importance of leveraging the strengths of your team

While all-stars are present in every organization, it is wise that your ministry operates with a belief that it is the sum of the parts that makes an organization successful. Every organization is like the body of Christ—it is made up of people with different talents, gifts, and strengths. One person won't have them all, so make sure you leverage the strengths of your team members in areas where you may be weak. Be humble about your weaknesses, work to improve them, and position your organization for success by identifying and leveraging the strengths of others.

Lesson #5: The importance of knowing what you don't know

Nobody likes a know-it-all. The temptation to act like you are an expert on something when you really aren't is usually the result of insecurity. If you don't know the answer to a question or what to do in a certain situation, be content with the fact that it's okay. In most instances, there is time to ask someone who does. By being honest about what you know and don't know, you will strengthen your credibility and increase the respect that others have for you.

Lesson #6: The importance of having a broader understanding beyond your job description

If a person working in an entry level position only understands their role, they will underestimate the value of their job and how it fits into the bigger picture. Whether it is through new employee training programs or through personally taking initiative, make sure you understand how your role impacts others and how your role is helping execute your ministry's vision and mission. Having this understanding creates a higher sense of purpose and will enable you to create more value for your ministry.

Lesson #7: The importance of communication—follow up and follow through

Similar to punctuality, if you don't follow up and follow through, your credibility will be damaged—no matter who you are. It's one of the easiest and most fundamental interpersonal skills, yet most people struggle with it. If you make a commitment, follow through on it. If you're going to miss a deadline, give the recipient proper notice to reset expectations. If you miss a call or receive an email/text, respond promptly or at least let the person know you received their communication and provide the adequate response as soon as you are able. These two simple, fundamental skills heavily influence an organization's culture and reputation. You want your organization to be known as one that responds quickly, responds accurately, and follows through on all commitments in a timely manner. Commit to doing it—it's all within your control.

Lesson #8: The importance of treating everyone with the same respect

When I started my career as a project manager at SPS, I incorrectly thought I could treat suppliers with less respect than customers because I was paying them to provide me with a product or service. While that wasn't the right mindset to have, many businesses operate this way. Today, individuals and organizations have access to more information and options than ever before. The authors of the book, *Now, Build a Great Business*, suggest that the way to show everyone the same amount of respect is to "treat them like volunteers."[25] Operating with this mindset will change how you interact with others and ensure that you are treating everyone with the same amount of due respect.

Lesson #9: The importance of properly managing finances

Working in project management and sales has enabled me to have extensive hands-on experience with budgeting, profitability, and revenue forecasting. While finance can be intimidating, it is very simple at its fundamental levels. If you can add, subtract, multiply, and divide, you can properly manage finances. Get comfortable using programs like Microsoft Excel to create project budgets, cost projections, required funds, use of funds, profits and losses, and more. Treat the money your ministry has as if it is your own, and you will do what it takes to properly manage it.

Lesson #10: The importance of documenting processes

In every organization, so much information is discussed and used every day. If there are tasks that happen regularly (more than once), document them and create a process. If the same tasks are completed differently every time due to a lack of process standardization, your organization will never operate at its full potential. Identify what information needs to be documented, keep it organized, keep it updated, and work towards standardizing your operating procedures as much as possible.

Lesson #11: The importance of doing things you don't like with excellence

Nearly every job has trade-offs. There are positives and negatives to everything. If you want to differentiate yourself and your ministry, do the things you don't like with excellence. No matter what the task, with God as your audience, everything can be a form of worship.

Lesson #12: The importance of leading yourself

In his book, *Results Based Leadership*, author David Ulrich defines the effective leadership formula as follows: "Attributes x Results = Effective Leadership."[26] This means that individuals must have the right attributes (competencies, experience, and personality traits) and must generate the right results in order to be effective leaders. If your role is at the entry level of your ministry, you are not expected to lead others, but you are expected to lead yourself. In John Maxwell's book, *The 360 Degree Leader*, he states

---

[25] Mark Thompson and Brian Tracy, *Now, Build a Great Business* (New York City: AMACOM, 2011), 9.

[26] David Ulrich, et al, *Results Based Leadership* (Boston: Harvard Business School Press, 1999), 3.

that you are to "lead yourself exceptionally well,"[27] which will position you to effectively lead others. Regardless of your role, understand the results required of you and develop the necessary attributes to consistently achieve them. You will then successfully lead yourself and others in executing your ministry's vision and mission.

Lesson Learned #13: The importance of taking initiative

It's been said that no question is a foolish question. For the most part that is true, especially if the question is asked with a sincere desire to learn. Be bold in your desire to understand what you don't know. By doing so, your confidence will increase and you will create additional capabilities to strengthen your team.

Lesson Learned #14: The importance of thinking correctly and having the proper perspective

In the book, *Telling Yourself the Truth*, author William Backus states that no matter what circumstances you face, what you tell yourself in either words or attitude, will dictate your feelings and actions. He calls this "self talk."[28] How you think about and interpret the events around you dictates how you feel about them. How you feel determines how you act. If you perceive a task or circumstance in a way that makes you fearful or anxious, there's a chance that by learning more about it or by interpreting it differently, your initial perception will change. This is easier said than done, but it is true for nearly every circumstance you face. If all else fails, look at what you are experiencing with an eternal perspective. The right perspective creates hope, and it is hope that enables us to look beyond difficulties.

Lesson Learned #15: Understanding that everything you do matters

Everything that you experience and learn compounds. Nothing is wasted and God can use it all. Even if something seems mundane (and even pointless), the skills you are acquiring may be critical for future opportunities. If we do everything for the Lord, He can use it all for His purposes.

---

[27] John Maxwell, *The 360 Degree Leader* (Nashville: Thomas Nelson, Inc., 2005), 84.

[28] William Backus and Marie Chapian, *Telling Yourself The Truth* (Bloomington: Bethany House Publishers, 1980, 1981, 2000), 28.

Book References

1. Aaker, David, *Developing Business Strategies*
2. Backus, William, and Chapian, Marie, *Telling Yourself The Truth*
3. Block, Peter, *Flawless Consulting*
4. Carnegie, Dale, *How To Win Friends and Influence People*
5. Collins, Jim, *Good to Great*
6. Drucker, Peter, *Management Tasks, Responsibilities, Practices*
7. D'Souza, Sean, *The Brain Audit*
8. Freese, A. Thomas, *Question Based Selling*
9. Friga N., Paul, *The McKinsey Engagement*
10. Gerber E., Michael, *E-Myth Mastery*
11. Goleman, Daniel, *Emotional Intelligence*
12. Maxwell, John, *The 360 Degree Leader*
13. McGrath Gunther, Rita and MacMillan, Ian, *The Entrepreneurial Mindset*
14. Osterwalder, Alexander and Pigneur, Yves, *Business Model Generation*
15. Silvoso, Ed, *Anointed For Business*
16. The Barna Group, www.barna.org – *Churchless*
17. Thompson, Mark and Tracy, Brian, *Now, Build a Great Business*
18. Ulrich, David, *Results Based Leadership*
19. VanAuken, Brad, *Brand Aid*

A Final Note...

If you and your ministry have benefitted from this book, please email *The Smart Ministry* team at **contact@thesmartministry.com**. We would be honored to share your testimonial on our website. Thank you!

CPSIA information can be obtained at www.ICGtesting.com
Printed in the USA
BVOW09*1827110116

431747BV00009B/9/P